GET
FINANCIALLY
NAKED

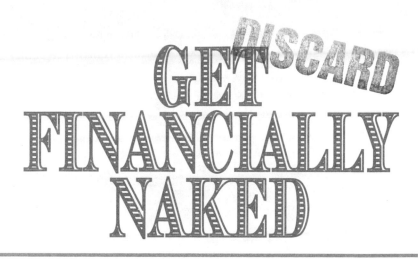

GET FINANCIALLY NAKED

HOW TO TALK MONEY *with your honey*

INCLUDES THE FIVE POWER STEPS TO FINANCIAL SUCCESS!

MANISHA THAKOR, MBA, CFA, AND
SHARON KEDAR, MBA, CFA,
authors of *On My Own Two Feet*

BUSINESS

Avon, Massachusetts

Published by Adams Business,
an imprint of Adams Media, a division of F+W Media, Inc.
57 Littlefield Street, Avon, MA 02322. U.S.A.
www.adamsmedia.com

ISBN 10: 1-4405-0201-3
ISBN 13: 978-1-4405-0201-9

Printed in the United States of America.

10 9 8 7 6 5 4 3 2 1

3 1540 00313 2683

Library of Congress Cataloging-in-Publication Data
is available from the publisher.

This publication is designed to provide accurate and authoritative information with regard to the subject matter covered. It is sold with the understanding that the publisher is not engaged in rendering legal, accounting, or other professional advice. If legal advice or other expert assistance is required, the services of a competent professional person should be sought.
　　—From a *Declaration of Principles* jointly adopted by a Committee of the American Bar Association and a Committee of Publishers and Associations

Many of the designations used by manufacturers and sellers to distinguish their product are claimed as trademarks. Where those designations appear in this book and Adams Media was aware of a trademark claim, the designations have been printed with initial capital letters.

This book is available at quantity discounts for bulk purchases.

For information, please call 1-800-289-0963.

To All Women

Contents

PART B TALKING MONEY WITH YOUR HONEY ... 51

PART C TIME TO GET TACTICAL...105

What This Book Can Do for You

Get *Financially Naked* will empower you to live the life that makes your heart sing—on your own and in the context of your romantic relationship. How on earth, you may ask, can a book about money do all that?

First, this book will help you and your partner get on the same financial page, which means your relationship is much less likely to get torpedoed by financial stress. Second, by learning to talk about money with your honey in a constructive way, the odds are high that you will dramatically strengthen your relationship. Time and again, we've seen how getting intimate with this traditionally taboo subject is one of the best investments you can make in your relationship. This book will not only help you decide who will handle which financial responsibilities, but it will also help you dramatically increase your odds of achieving household financial harmony.

When we say "Get Financially Naked," we mean learning to discuss the subject of money with your partner in a constructive way and learning to make smart decisions together about how to handle your personal finances. This book provides you the roadmap, language, and tactical tools to talk successfully about money with your honey.

We fully recognize that most people don't like to deal with their personal finances. So here's the good news: money is merely an enabler. The result, the real gift of Getting Financially Naked, is the ability to have a life that makes you want to jump out of bed in the morning and twirl around in joy. That's how this book about money can help you achieve your dream life.

Interestingly, we didn't plan to write this book. Rather, it jumped out at us and asked to be brought into existence. As we traveled across the country to promote our first book, a personal finance primer titled *On My Own Two Feet: A Modern Girl's Guide to Personal Finance,* we were surprised to find that the chapter to which women were most drawn was one we almost didn't include—a short discussion about love and money. In our typical speech on Personal Finance 101, we'd point out that if you are willing to disrobe one way in a committed relationship, you should be willing to disrobe financially as well. This statement would typically evoke nervous laughter from the crowd and more than a handful of flushed faces. So we'd always go on to clarify that we're NOT talking about doing this on the first date. We'd emphasize:

> Getting Financially Naked is something you do when you are in a serious, committed relationship.

We'd explain that this process entails discussing money with your mate. Specifically, it involves discussing what you own, what you owe, your income, and what your credit scores are before moving in together or getting married. Getting Financially Naked is not limited to what you earn, spend, and save. It's also about understanding your respective hopes and fears regarding money—a process that goes way beyond raw numbers. Most importantly, financially baring it all is not a one-time activity. It involves regular check-ins as a couple to make sure you are meeting your savings goals, investing wisely, that you both know where your important papers are stored, and seeing if any of your life priorities have changed. As we'd say all this in our presentations, heads would inevitably start to bob gently up and down in agreement. And once our speech would end, it would start.

Woman after woman would come up to tell us how she wished she'd heard our speech or read *On My Own Two Feet* earlier. We'd hear stories about women in relationships where they, their mate, or both of them, mismanaged money, or they simply didn't agree about how to manage money. Even worse, we'd hear stories from women who thought everything was fine when it came to each of their family's money situation, but the reality was far from it. These women had all been short-changed when it came to their money and their relationships. It's no wonder. When you meet that someone special, what do your friends ask you? They ask if you are emotionally, physically, and spiritually compatible. However, consider this:

When was the last time someone asked if you were financially compatible with your mate?

Probably never. Study after study shows that money is one of the top causes of arguments in marriages, top reasons for divorce, and top drivers of general life stress. If you are thinking this couldn't happen to you or someone you know and love, think again. The women we met are representative of *every* woman. She is everyone from a woman with a graduate degree in business working in high finance to a newly minted high school graduate who has never had her own credit card. What we've discovered on the road is that getting the short end of the stick in a relationship, financially speaking, has absolutely no connection to your educational, economic, social, or ethnic background. We've seen it happen to every type of woman imaginable.

Now, we're not suggesting that women should be distrustful of their mates or adopt a victim mentality. If we had focused our financial literacy efforts on men, we have no doubt we'd hear comparable stories from their side. Our point is simply that across America, we are hearing stories of financial distress—and many of these situations could have been prevented by frank and honest dialogue about money.

The Need for This Book

To give you a sense of where we're coming from, here are just a few of the tales we were told:

- **Haley:** The established doctor whose husband started a business that went down the toilet, taking their family's home equity and net worth along the way. If it weren't for the last minute help of a generous extended family member they would have literally lost the roof over their heads.

- **Anika:** The newlywed who can't stop fighting with her husband over money, something they never even talked about when they were dating. When she asked about funding a spousal Individual Retirement Account (IRA) for her, her husband responded, "Why, are you thinking of leaving me?"
- **Nicole:** The stay-at-home mom who wants to spend some money taking the children to travel and broaden their horizons but fights with her husband because he thinks that's not a good use of their joint funds at this point in time and won't allow it.
- **Beverly:** The young, smart, urban professional who co-signed a loan with her former boyfriend—and is still paying off her half of the debt despite the fact he's long gone from her life.
- **Kit:** The experienced family law professional whose day-trading spouse took the household's hard earned savings and gambled it away—all while she watched, without the heart to tell him to stop. Now, at age sixty, she's divorced and starting all over again from financial ground zero.

We met these bright women all across the country. So what happened? How did they end up in this place of financial angst? Why did they hand over their financial power? Typically, the answer is simple. They avoided the topic of money because they either found the subject matter painfully boring and/or they wanted to avoid an awkward conversation or another fight. In fact, we'd venture to guess that at least one woman you know, if not more, could join this list right now. Think about that for a moment. Even if money is not an immediate source of stress to you, could any of your close friends or family members be in a place of angst with their household finances? Could any of the strong women you know be giving up control of their finances—and therefore their lives—to their mate?

The good news is that together we can and will put a stop to this situation. Fighting about money and/or allowing it to destroy a relationship are completely avoidable situations. So with this book we are putting out a call to action for all women. Despite the phenomenal strides women have made in all walks of life, we are still seeing too many women hand over the financial reins to others. So what's the answer?

Enter *Get Financially Naked*. The goal of this book is threefold:

1. To show you how to define the financial life of your dreams.
2. To teach you how to talk with your honey in an empowering, collaborative way about the key financial decisions most couples face.
3. To present you with the tactical tools to create your joint financial plan and achieve your financial dream life.

Financial compatibility is one of the greatest predictors of whether your relationship will survive long term. This book will help you achieve that success.

The Layout of This Book

This book is divided into three parts. In the first section, you will learn the benefits of Owning Your Finances and Owning Your Life. We'll help you get to know your naked financial self and identify your dream financial life. This is a critical step. Just as you can't really love someone else until you first love yourself—you can't get your household finances in order until you have a positive relationship with money. We'll also show you how to get an initial sense of where your mate is coming from, financially.

In the second section of the book we will tell you exactly when and how to discuss the topic of money with your mate. Many women have told us they'd like to have a "script" to help them handle this conversation. That's why we kick off Part B of the book with a financial compatibility quiz for you and your mate to do and discuss. The purpose of this quiz is to help you both understand your areas of compatibility and areas of potential strife. This is important knowledge that you can use to talk constructively about what's coming next—the "Five Power Steps to Financial Success." If you get these five steps right, you'll be well on your way to financial nirvana.

In the third and final section of the book, we will help you move forward by providing tactical tools for saving and investing that will help you turn your financial dreams into reality. The culmination of this final section is the creation of your personal financial plan.

The best part is . . .

You don't have to love (or even like) dealing with money for this book to improve your life.

One of the most common questions we got with our first book, *On My Own Two Feet*, was "Why focus on women?" We're betting more than a few people will ask the same about *Get Financially Naked*. While the advice in this book absolutely will help both genders, we once again dedicated this book "to all women." We want all women to feel entitled to own their finances.

Did you know that 80 percent of men die married while 80 percent of women die single?

Shocking, right? This figure is primarily a result of women's longer life spans; we live an average of seven years longer than men do. Another contributing factor is our nation's roughly 50 percent divorce rate and the tendency of older men, in particular, to remarry more frequently than older women. Combine this with the trend toward women marrying later in life—if at all—and the result is that 90 percent of American women will find themselves as the sole provider of their personal finances at some point in their adult lives. This is why it is so important for us women to get involved with our money now, before a crisis hits. It's much easier—and a whole lot more fun—to proactively and confidently take control of your finances now, rather than wait until life has just slapped you in the face and all you can do is react.

Financial knowledge is the ultimate gift that a woman can give herself.

Women aren't the only ones who will benefit from this book. *Get Financially Naked* will help both women and men, as it will drastically reduce the number of money-related fights and stress about money. For couples all across America, money has become the pink elephant in the bedroom, the subject dealt with every day on the surface but not delved into in a truly intimate, respectful way. *Get Financially Naked* will help you by eliminating money as a source of stress in your life and in your relationships. So turn the page, and join us on the journey to financial knowledge and empowerment.

PART A

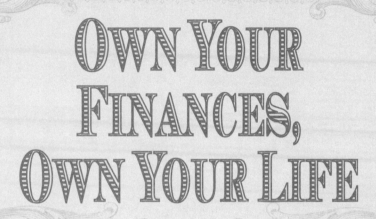

OWN YOUR FINANCES, OWN YOUR LIFE

CHAPTER ONE

Get Financially Naked

If you want to achieve financial satisfaction with your honey, you must first understand how to achieve it on your own. When you think about it, this makes perfect sense. If you do not know what makes you happy, how on earth can you expect someone else to help support you on the path to get there? That's why Getting Financially Naked with yourself is the critical first step toward achieving a lifetime of financial compatibility with your mate.

Millions of people find the mere thought of dealing with their personal finances overwhelming. Often this is because they think that good personal financial hygiene must be complicated or involve a lot of tedious math or accounting. Ironically, the most important personal finance steps are quite basic. The payoff from taking these steps is tremendous.

> When you learn the basics of personal finance and have your financial house in order, you can make major life decisions from a position of strength.

You can make career and relationship decisions for the right reasons. You can pursue the interests and hobbies that put a real spring in your step. Moreover, you can sidestep the risk of someone sabotaging your dreams and hard work. In other words, you are squarely behind the steering wheel of your life. While you may run into twists and turns along the way, you are in the driver's seat. Let's get this journey started by looking at what you get when you are on top of your money. Here are some examples of what financial empowerment means to several women:

WHAT FINANCIAL EMPOWERMENT MEANS TO ME . . .

"Financial empowerment means choices, freedom, independence. Choices in how I provide for myself and those I love and give to my community. Freedom to be in charge of my life. Independence to pursue my dreams." —Gloria

"Financial empowerment means that I can take care of myself and those I care about, I can choose a healthy business or personal relationship, I can be aware of how the bills are paid rather than worry about how the bills are paid." —Lisa

"Financial empowerment means having choices . . . about what you do, where you live, and how you spend your time." —Evelyn

Financial empowerment means I can take care of myself and my family financially. It means I can support the causes I believe in. It means I can walk away from a bad situation at work or at home if necessary. It means I can buy a dress without having to check with anyone." —Sheila

"Financial empowerment means the freedom to be, do, and have what I want and to make the greatest contribution to the world." —Brenda

A World Gone Wild . . . Financially Speaking

Think of the last time you were around a group of people of varying ages—this could be at your office, the movies, a restaurant, in the grocery store, or just walking down the street. Now here's a startling statistic: if it was a typical group of Americans,

5

seven out of every ten of those people are living essentially paycheck-to-paycheck, according to the American Payroll Association. Believe it or not, this unfortunate reality cuts across income lines.

If the whole world Got Financially Naked, you'd likely be amazed at how many people making six figures and even seven figures (yes, seven figures) are living from one paycheck to the next.

This means that 70 percent of us are living one payday away from financial chaos. Keep this in mind the next time you go out, and chances are you will begin to view things from a completely new perspective. For instance, take that guy cruising by in a shiny new sports car. Perhaps it's the biggest asset he's got. Or take the woman wearing the latest designer jeans and carrying a trendy handbag. Maybe she'll be paying those off on her credit card for the next thirty years. Our point is that for many, many people the odds are high that the image they project to the outside world does not match the reality of their income and net worth.

Why are so many of us living from one paycheck to the next? There are three key reasons. First, many of us lack a clear roadmap, which means we're driving blind when it comes to our money. How did this happen? Because personal finance, like parenting, is one of those skills that we are expected to simply pick up "along the way." We are not formally taught the basics of it, and unlike parenting, there is not much societal support for admitting to monetary confusion. As a result, many of us end up deciding what is "right and normal" based on the spending habits of *others*. Let's talk about that for a moment.

Think about your neighbors. Do you ever wonder how it all adds up? Have you ever found yourself wondering how they can afford that house, that car, those vacations, that school, those clothes?

Given that so many Americans are living essentially pay-check-to-paycheck, the chances are high that for at least some of your neighbors, you're right: the numbers do not add up. If you can't quite figure out how your neighbors seem to "afford" to pay for all that they have and do, it may very well be that they are funding those expenditures with debt. Millions of Americans spend more than they earn, using debt to make up the difference.

Second, it's not just the neighbors on your street living beyond their means. Turn on the TV and you'll see all sorts of people—fictional and real—who are living financial fantasy lives. Have you ever met a law enforcement professional who was able to dress as sharply as those on *NCIS* and *Law & Order* or a doctor in residency who was able to afford (let alone have time for) the kinds of personal grooming clearly going on in shows like *House* and *Grey's Anatomy*? How many middle-class housewives do you know who live like the women on *Desperate Housewives*? And how real are the lives on *The Bachelor* anyway? In other words, we are bombarded with media images of "average" lifestyles that are anything but.

The third, and most critical, factor has been easy access to credit. Up until the credit crisis of 2008–2009, we could all dash to the mailbox in our pajamas, rip open a credit card application, and we were off to the spending races. Before financial institutions became so lax, if you wanted to borrow money, you had to put on your Sunday finest, march down to your local bank, and have a long chat with the loan officer. You were forced to explain what that money would be used for and how you would pay it back. And in years past, regulation was such that lenders had to charge everyone the same interest rate. So if you were a bad risk, they just wouldn't lend to you. Period. That's not true anymore and because of changes in regulations, lenders can now "tier" the interest rates they offer consumers. That means if you are a high risk, you can still get credit— they'll just charge you more (usually much more) for it.

> Most people assume they will only be offered credit if they can "afford it." All too often it's the reverse; being offered a lot of credit is frequently a sign that lenders think they can make a lot of money off you.

Given this backdrop, it's really no surprise people get in over their heads financially. If this happens when someone is single, the odds are high it will be even more pronounced in the context of a relationship. As we mentioned in the introduction, time and again, money is cited as the #1 cause of fights in relationships and stress in general. For example, in a recent *Money Magazine* poll, 85 percent of respondents reported that money is causing tension in their marriages. The good news is that it does not have to be this way. By the time you are finished reading *Get Financially Naked*, you will have the tools to make money a powerful, positive aspect of your life.

Where to Start?

When you live your life from a position of financial strength, you are able to spend your time and energy the way you want to. You are able to pursue the types of work and activities that truly make your heart sing. Living your life from a position of financial strength starts with knowing where you want to go financially. The reality is that most Americans do not think about their monetary goals. However, in this financial world gone wild, it's never been more important to have a clear vision of what you want. We'd like you to respond to the following sentence with whatever comes to mind: "When I live my life from a position of financial strength, I will . . ." Simply write down whatever—and we really do mean *whatever*—pops into your head.

If you've never done an exercise like this before, here are a few pointers. There are no right or wrong answers, and nothing is off limits. This exercise is all about uncovering the authentic you. Simply look at the phrase "When I live my life from a position of financial strength, I will . . ." and let your pen start moving across the page. You may find yourself jotting down words, phrases, feelings, or full sentences—whatever bubbles up is great.

When I live my life from a position of financial strength, I will . . .

_____

_____

_____

_____

_____

_____

_____

_____

To remind yourself of where you are heading, please copy or paste your responses to this visualization exercise on the front inside cover of this book—and anywhere else you like around your house. (You can download extra copies at *www.GetFinanciallyNaked.com*.)

We encourage you to refresh your response to this visualization exercise as your life circumstances evolve. Manisha likes to review hers every January as part of her New Year's resolution ritual. Sharon likes to do hers more spontaneously. You decide what works best for you. The main reason to periodically go back to this exercise is that as you start to see the incredible freedom that comes with getting on top of your money, you are likely to find that your dreams and hopes—and the steps you take—get bigger and bolder. We've seen it time and again with women who truly commit to Getting Financially Naked.

Having done this exercise with countless women, we've noticed that some feel surprised or embarrassed about what they have written down. We want to emphasize this very important point: The objective of this exercise is not to judge the quality of your answers, but rather to be completely truthful and deliberately nonjudgmental with yourself.

Whether you want to go on a luxurious vacation or build a school in a third-world country, the key is to know what makes your heart sing. The reason this visualization exercise is so powerful is that once you know what you want out of your life, you can then make sure your financial actions are in line with your vision. Our only counsel is this: aim high. Don't put any limitations on yourself. Want what you want. Any vision is achievable with commitment.

MANISHA AND SHARON'S RESPONSES TO THE VISUALIZATION EXERCISE

In the spirit of Getting Financially Naked, remember that sharing your vision with friends can be very empowering. Time and again, we've seen the incredible magic that occurs when a group of women share their visions with each other. Go for it. We highly recommend inviting a group of women over for drinks and sharing your responses. We'll help get you started. Following are our answers to the visualization exercise.

MANISHA'S VISUALIZATION

- *Live with my incredible husband in a not-too-big contemporary home that has beautiful views of nature*
- *Be in complete charge of my days—no more mind-numbing corporate meetings!*
- *Earn an emotionally and financially healthy living as a personal finance expert for women*
- *Be able to help my family and contribute to the causes I believe in*
- *Have the freedom to hang out in cafés reading, writing, and just thinking*
- *Exercise regularly, eat healthy and delicious foods, and have family and friends over for wonderful meals and inspiring chats*
- *Travel to interesting places with my husband; experiencing together the simple, small joys of daily life and new adventures*

SHARON'S VISUALIZATION

- *Strike a healthy balance between being a mother, business professional, and financial literacy advocate*
- *Have time for myself and the financial freedom to do what I want*
- *Work because I want to, and do what really makes me happy*
- *Take fun family vacations that bring our extended family together several times a year*
- *Be able to use my position of financial strength to make a difference and improve the lives of others*
- *Be able to indulge myself when I want—with a massage or a little luxury*

Turning Your Visualization into Reality

If you wonder how on earth you can achieve your visualization, please know that over and over again we've seen how the power of time and commitment can make it possible. If you set your mind to it, you can get there. We are highly practical people, and thus we don't say this lightly: Anything is possible, even if you don't know today exactly how you'll get there. You can do this. No matter where you are starting and no matter how tough your current situation may feel, it is possible to get on your own two feet, financially speaking. If you feel overwhelmed or confused—you are not alone. Many before you have felt the exact same way.

Take Martina, for instance. For years, Martina worked diligently as a nurse—earning a healthy salary, maintaining good credit, and buying her own home. Then she married a man who, unbeknownst to her, was her financial opposite. Long story short, this man had a strong "get rich quick" gene in him. Things *seemed* okay until he decided to open up his own construction business and move the family to a bigger house. Martina trusted him to handle the finances. She was busy working and raising their two kids. She didn't check their bills closely and before she knew it, things had taken a turn for the worse. Their big, new house went into foreclosure, unpaid credit card debt piled up, creditors hounded them, and the final kicker— Martina found out that her husband had been cheating on her for years.

Suffice it to say, they are now separated. Martina is strong, tough, and determined not to let this piece of her life history repeat itself. That's a big part of the reason Martina allowed us to share her story. Not only has she learned from this experience, but she hopes that many other women will too. Money never really interested her until she was at a point in her life where she almost lost it all. She hopes you never reach that place.

MARTINA'S RESPONSE TO: "WHEN I LIVE MY LIFE FROM A POSITION OF FINANCIAL STRENGTH, I WILL . . ."

- *Take a Disneyland Cruise . . . because I've never been to Disneyland*

- *Have money to take care of my kids and take them on nice vacations*
- *Have FUN with my life . . . and get a new pair of shoes or jeans when I want*

If you are determined to live your life from a place of financial strength, you can get there no matter what the obstacles. To illustrate this point, we'd like to tell you about another woman, Sandra. Sandra was a foster child who was adopted at an early age and grew up living below the poverty line. However, from a young age, Sandra had a crystal-clear vision of what she wanted. She was determined to change her reality and improve her situation, and thus worked hard from a very young age. Today she lives her life from a position of financial strength, with a loving family and a successful career. Here is her story:

Sandra's Story . . . in Her Own Words

"Like many of us, my family did not have much money growing up. My mother raised my brother and me on a secretary's salary, which was not much. My mom was not able to hide from us the fact that money was tight in the family—in fact, our financial situation seemed to dominate every decision. For example, we were always dressed in second-hand clothes from garage sales and second-hand stores. We knew where to go to get a good deal. Shirts were fifty cents, shoes were $2. And I hated my wardrobe.

I remember when I was in high school and I was a competitive public speaker, a judge wrote on one of my feedback forms that I needed to 'dress better' and 'get a haircut.' Most people didn't realize when I was in high school, and later on in college, how hard I had to work to keep my grades up and do all of the activities I loved doing. The rule in our house was once we were old enough to work at something (read: thirteen years old), we had to pay our own way for things. Play soccer? Go on that school trip? Get a job. When I was twenty years old I made a list of every 'job' I had had up to that point. I counted eighteen separate places of employment—most of the time I was working two to three jobs to piece together enough money to pay for rent, car insurance, and food.

Today, I am in my mid-thirties, financially secure, with a great career. That said, in my personal life, it is hard to get away from the fear of not having money—of losing it all. My husband and I live in a nice neighborhood, our kids are well fed and clothed, and we are saving for retirement and college. However, my history with money always leaves me ill at ease and thinking that it could all go away. I view money as the key to independence—the ability to make decisions for yourself."

SANDRA'S RESPONSE TO: "WHEN I LIVE MY LIFE FROM A POSITION OF FINANCIAL STRENGTH, I WILL . . ."

- *When I live from a position of financial strength, I will be secure in meeting my family's present and future needs, and have the ability to create room in my life to focus on enjoying my family and friends in my "downtime."*

- *My children will be happy and healthy, and my relationships will be fueled by personal, positive interactions.*

Talk the Talk, Walk the Walk

Once you have stated your visualization, it's time to take action. Getting on top of your money is like the financial equivalent of putting on your oxygen mask. If you've ever flown in an airplane, you know that the flight attendants always remind you, "In the event of an emergency, put your oxygen mask on first before helping those around you." The same goes when it comes to your money. When you take care of your finances first, you are in a much better position to help the people, causes, and organizations that are important to you. That's why this book about money and relationships starts off with a detailed discussion focused on you.

So far, you'll note there have been no numbers or calculations in our conversation. While economic experts will throw percentages, stats, and charts at us—the truth is they're often hard to identify with. The good news is that they are often irrelevant. Living a healthy financial life does not have to be complicated. To achieve financial success, you do not need to understand foreign currency derivatives or how to identify which company will become the next Google. In fact, history shows that, more often than not, "keep-it-simple" is the best strategy. This means that if you do not understand a piece of financial advice, you should feel empowered to ask for clarification. If you still don't understand, don't do it. To truly live your life from a position of financial strength, you must stay true to yourself and act from an informed position.

Perhaps the best news of all is that you don't even need to like the details of personal finance to be successful at it.

Take the two of us, for example. While we are both MBAs and chartered financial analysts who have worked in the financial services industry for years—that's where our similarities end when it comes to money. Manisha loves the minutiae of money and thinks it is fun to read personal finance books. Sharon, by contrast, really finds the details of personal finance boring— and frequently says so when giving speeches. However, both of us are living our lives from a position of financial strength—by getting the few really important things right. We'll repeat this over and over:

Personal finance can and should be simple. What really matters is to understand and act on the "big stuff."

Once you have finished reading this book, you will know what that big stuff is and how to act on it in a keep-it-simple manner.

Own Your Finances, Own Your Life

As you venture out to live from a position of financial strength, we want you to remember two key points. The first is that this book is not really about money. It's about leading the life you want to lead. The empowerment of our fellow females to live the life they want is what gets us so excited and passionate about the subject of financial literacy. As we like to say, "Own Your Finances, Own Your Life."

The second key point is, while every single step will not be easy or fun, by keeping your answers to the visualization exercise in mind, you can find the inner strength to stay on the path. We say this from personal experience. Here are just a couple of recent examples from our lives to make this point.

Sharon went to the store the other day to buy a sweater. After selecting a sweater, the salesperson brought over a jacket and said, "Try this on." Sharon asked, "How much does it cost?" The salesperson repeated, "Just try it on." Committed to staying on her budget, Sharon asked again, "But how much does it cost?" The salesperson side-stepped her query by responding that the item was on sale. Finally Sharon looked the woman right in the eyes and said, "Can you please tell me how much this costs *before* I try it on?" The woman finally went to scan the item to find out its price. Turns out, the jacket was indeed out of her budget, so Sharon did not even try it on. Stunned by this interaction, Sharon called Manisha and said, "Wow, people need to hear about this experience. We've got to encourage people to speak up and protect themselves!"

Not long after, Manisha was in a restaurant and the waiter asked if she would like to hear the specials. Manisha said yes, and the waiter proceeded to rattle off a list of mouth-watering dishes. One of them was the fish of the day, and it sounded delicious. Knowing that fresh fish dishes can be expensive, Manisha asked, "How much does it cost?" The waiter stared back at her with wide eyes. After a long, awkward pause he finally said, "Gosh, I don't know. Let me go find out." He returned with the price, and it was almost 50 percent more than the regular dinner entrées. Manisha didn't order it.

Ready to Bare All?

The temptation to stray is everywhere. From time to time, you will stumble because you are human. It's okay. After you pick yourself up and dust yourself off, remind yourself why you are taking the steps you are regarding your finances. Staying rooted in *your* goals is the key to staying on track.

Get Financially Naked will help you find your path. If you remember to look within and stay focused on your life vision, you will not only achieve your dreams but inspire others to do so as well. When you "Own Your Finances" you really can "Own Your Life."

THE POWER OF FRIENDSHIP

If you want the added support, we encourage you to take those girlfriends you invited over to share your financial visualization and go a step further. Create a Financial Empowerment Club to provide support as you work through this book. Check out *www.GetFinanciallyNaked .com* to download a guidebook for your club.

CHAPTER TWO

Uncover Your Current Financial Beliefs

Your attitude about money is one of the key driving forces behind your success with money. If you are not where you want to be today, financially, it's likely the result of your current financial beliefs.

If you are like most people, you are probably thinking, "But I don't have any defined 'beliefs' about money." This is a common misperception. Money is one of those things—like breathing or blinking—that is part of everybody's daily life in one way or another. Whether it's the toast you had for breakfast, the shoes you put on for work, the pen you used to write a note, the cup of tea you had with a friend in the afternoon, or the home you came back to at the end of the day, money was involved to allow those items and experiences to appear in your life. Over the course of a lifetime, the average person has countless interactions with money. At the same time, people are constantly observing how others deal with money. Cumulatively, all of these observations come together to create your personal money history. That money history in turn has shaped what we call your current financial beliefs.

> Your current financial beliefs are like a series of short recordings in your head that influence your every interaction with money—for better or for worse.

Your current financial beliefs may be conscious or unconscious. If you find that they are at odds with your overarching life goals, you'll find yourself mentally blocked. You can observe a similar dynamic at work in many other areas of your life. Take food for instance. You may have perceptions, memories, or emotional responses to food that give it meaning way beyond nutritional sustenance. In the same vein, you may have comparable thoughts and feelings about money that elevate it beyond a means of paying for things. The next step in Getting Financially Naked is to review your money history to uncover (and potentially adjust) your resulting current financial beliefs. To connect effectively with your partner about your finances, you'll first want to make sure your beliefs and goals are in balance.

To illustrate that your attitude must align with your goals, we'd like to tell you about Amy. When Amy did the exercise in Chapter 1 (the one where we asked you to finish the phrase "When I live my life from a position of financial strength, I will . . ."), she responded that she wanted to have enough money so she didn't ever have to worry about it. Yet in practice, one of Amy's current underlying beliefs about money is "Live for today since you can't take it with you." As such, it's possible Amy may never achieve her financial dreams. Why? The current financial belief she stated is in direct conflict with one of her goals. If Amy lives for today without balancing the need to save for tomorrow, she cannot truly live her life from a position of financial strength. To make meaningful progress toward her life dream, Amy will first need to be aware of her current financial beliefs. She must then ask herself if they need to be modified or rethought to reach her objectives.

Let's get started on a simple process that will help uncover your current financial beliefs.

Please write down whatever thoughts or feelings come to mind when you hear the word M-O-N-E-Y. Don't dwell on it; just write whatever pops into your head. Just as with the last exercise, allow yourself the freedom of being completely nonjudgmental about your answers. As you write, be as honest as you possibly can with yourself. No thought is off-limits.

_____

_____

_____

_____

Well done. You've just taken a significant step forward in your relationship with your money; you've been honest with yourself. You might be surprised to find out how many people are scared to do this. This is a powerful exercise because it shines a spotlight on your current underlying beliefs, some of which you may not have even known existed.

MONEY IS . . .

Money is a topic that stirs up many emotions. Here is a sampling of what other women have said when they think of the word M-O-N-E-Y.

- Yuck, I don't want to deal . . . I do deal, but I must admit, it's not a joy!
- Stress on one hand and freedom on the other.
- A source of anxiety.

- Freedom, luxury, power to do what I want, power to improve the world.
- Something to be earned and saved so that you can take care of yourself, the cause of most arguments, and a validation of my hard work.

The Magical Power of Money Histories

When it comes to money, your past really is more like a prologue. Your formative experiences have a tremendous influence on you. This was certainly true for us.

While growing up, we each came to believe that money enables independence for ourselves as individuals and ultimately for all women in general. However, the way in which we each arrived at that viewpoint was strikingly different. This helps highlight two key points about money histories. First, they are highly personal. Two people may draw similar conclusions from very different circumstances or entirely different conclusions from the exact same set of circumstances. Second, you have the power to take whatever happened in your past and reframe that history into a more empowering view of money. In other words, once you uncover your current financial beliefs, you have the power to *change* them.

In the following pages, the two of us share our individual money histories. We have done this so you can see the way in which highly personal influences and defining moments in each of our pasts came together to create our current views on money. Our paths are not inherently good or bad—they just are what they are. You will have your own unique and powerful story. It doesn't matter whether you struggled more or less than we did. It doesn't matter if you found money more or less interesting than we did growing up. In fact, we'd argue that the most unique part of each of our personal money histories is that we had an interest in the subject growing up (which probably explains why we ended up writing books about the topic!).

Manisha's Money History, in Her Own Words

When I think of the word M-O-N-E-Y, "freedom, independence, and life's small joys" come to mind. I'm definitely more focused on money than most people are. A big part of this is because I was one of those rare individuals who grew up in a household where money was talked about openly and honestly, and the basics of personal finance were taught. As a result, I love talking about money. Sometimes a bit too much! Saving and budgeting are my particular fortes. I can tell you accurately within $10 where every dollar I've spent since 1992 has gone. Geeky, even obsessive, I know. But it's what I need to do to feel financially confident.

My money history is defined by three key life experiences, explained on the following pages.

Growing Up a Dork. There really is no other way to put it. When I was in grade school, I was a smart, dorky looking girl. I had braces, coke-bottle glasses, a bad case of psoriasis (a skin condition), too much hair in places I wished it wouldn't grow, and a backside that caused the kids to dub me "cow butt." Ouch. I felt like the ultimate outsider. Not fitting in drove me to want to create a life for myself where I was in control. It made me want to be financially independent so I could lead the life I wanted to lead, surrounded by the people I chose to be with.

My Parents. They rock! My mom is an independent, forward-thinking woman. I am so proud of her. She went back to school in her fifties and got a PhD in biology. She now teaches at North Carolina State University. Growing up, my mother read gender-neutral books to me like *Free to Be You and Me*. My parents always encouraged me to be anything I wanted. When I graduated from college, my mother wrote me a beautiful letter advising me that I would face limitless choices as an adult, a constant tug between acquiring *things* and acquiring *experiences*. When in doubt, she advised going for the latter. Thus was born my desire to have the financial freedom to enjoy life's small joys. To be in a place where I have enough money to live life on my own terms, and not be bogged down with the quest for more and more things.

As for my dad, he is a financial genius. Literally. I'm so proud of him too. He grew up in India and came to the United States with the proverbial suitcase in hand and fire in his belly. From that modest start, he rose to become the chief financial officer of a Fortune 500 company. My dad always places family first. Despite a demanding career, he always makes time to share his knowledge with my brother and me. One of my pivotal personal money history moments was around age twelve when my dad had me calculate how much money I would have if I contributed $2,000 a year to my IRA until age sixty-five, and how that changed depending upon whether I earned 4 percent, 6 percent, 8 percent, or 10 percent on my investments. W-O-W, did my eyes pop open when I saw the incredible power of compounding. Thus was born my desire to start saving early in life so my money would have the most time to grow and compound.

Virginia Woolf. When I was in college, I spent my junior year at Oxford University. There I stumbled across a copy of Virginia Woolf's book *A Room of One's Own*. It literally changed my life. Written in the early 1900s, Woolf's argument is as relevant today as it was back then. In this delicious little book, she says that in order to fully realize one's talents and possibilities one must have "money and a room of one's own." Her argument that money gives women freedom to become their best selves has become my guiding mantra.

Combine these three forces—feeling like an outsider as a kid, the positive influence from my parents, and the feminist awakening triggered by Virginia Woolf's writings—and you end up with this: A woman who views money as an enabler, as a powerful tool that allows me to be myself and help the people and causes I care about.

Sharon's Money History, in Her Own Words

When I hear the word M-O-N-E-Y, I think of the word independence.

I am the child of immigrants. My father came to the United States with only an airplane ticket and very little money. He enrolled in engineering school in New Jersey and made his way from there. He met my mom while in school. She too was an immigrant without much money.

When I was born, my parents did not have health insurance. My father had just lost his job one month prior and had to pay for the birth of *twins*. Money was tight.

That said, growing up, I was a lucky kid. My dad ended up getting a job as a civil servant working for the U.S. government. My mom worked as a teacher and counselor, supplementing our family income. That meant that unlike my parents and grandparents, we always had food on the table and clothes on our backs. I remember being able to take the classes I wanted to, like ballet and swimming, and go on family vacations. Relative to the rest of the world, I had absolutely nothing to complain about.

However, I knew—even though we never talked about it explicitly—that money was tight and we needed to watch our dollars carefully. I was always an independent kid. So this frustrated me. At a very early age, I made a decision. Once I was capable, I was going to make enough so that money would never be the driving force in life decisions. This is because, from an early age, at first unconsciously and then consciously, I associated money with *independence*. That's why I started creating businesses at age five.

My first business was selling bookmarks with stickers (five cents) and "bear" magnets (twenty-five cents) to friends. I enlisted my twin sister to help me get the business going. We had quite a few more businesses as our childhood continued, including selling tie-dye outfits to friends in elementary school.

After high school (and multiple jobs that I won't bore you with between elementary school and high school), I went to college. I chose *Money Magazine's* "Best College Buy" at the time, Rice University, simply because of that status, and the knowledge that it would cost my parents the least amount of money. I knew I wanted a full-time job as soon as it made sense, and without piles of undergraduate student loans to pay off.

The vast majority of people do not grow up with a passion for learning about money. So do not think for a minute that you need to have been interested in money from a young age to be successful with your personal finances as an adult. Rather, the point we want to make is once you understand how your experiences influence your current relationship with money, you can *choose* to change your beliefs. Why might you want to do this? Again, it is only when your current financial beliefs are in harmony with your ultimate financial goals that you will become truly powerful with your money.

For those of you who dread the thought of having to deal with the nitty-gritty of your day-to-day finances, there's a bright light at the end of this tunnel to look forward to.

Once you have a powerful view of money that's in line with your financial goals, you can achieve financial success regardless of whether you want to be knee-deep in finances on a day-to-day basis.

In the coming chapters, we will help you assess your natural level of involvement, as well as your partner's, so you can set an approach to achieve your financial goals in a way that works best for you.

What's *Your* Money History?

Now it's your turn to Get Financially Naked. Getting real with yourself about your attitude toward money, where it came from, and how you want to either reinforce or change it is a powerful step to financial independence and success. It's time to dig a bit deeper into your underlying attitude about money. We've provided some questions to help stimulate the process. Feel free to pour yourself a glass of wine or whatever your choice beverage of relaxation is—these questions can tug at some intimate memories. (Note, if you'd like to download additional copies of this worksheet, go to *www.GetFinancially Naked.com.*)

How was money handled in your household when you were growing up? Who had the lead role?

_____

_____

_____

_____

_____

_____

Was money discussed growing up? What messages did you take away from how your family talked (or didn't talk) about money?

_____

_____

_____

_____

_____

_____

What is your worst memory that directly or indirectly involved money?

_____

_____

_____

_____

_____

_____

What is your best memory that directly or indirectly involved money?

_____

_____

_____

_____

_____

_____

How does the way in which money was handled and discussed in your household while you were growing up affect your life today?

_____

_____

_____

_____

_____

_____

Were you surprised by any of your answers? Many people are. These questions are intended to help you better understand your current behaviors and connect the dots. The goal is to shed some light on why your current situation is the way it is and how it was shaped by your direct and indirect experiences with money. For instance, when we talk about saving, you may realize that one reason you can't stay out of the stores is that you are rebelling against a childhood restraint. Or the reason you are afraid to invest is that you observed your parents having a bad experience with investing. This honest assessment of your past is the first step toward moving forward with your desired financial life.

Uncovering Your Current Financial Beliefs

Now, let's switch gears and pull this all together into something actionable. It's time to list your current financial beliefs, just as Amy did when she said people need to "live for today since you can't take it with you." As with the visualization exercise, no thought is off limit. Close your eyes, take a few deep breaths, and when you open your eyes, start writing down *anything* that comes to your mind.

When it comes to money, I believe that . . .

_____

_____

_____

_____

_____

_____

_____

_____

_____

You've just identified your current financial beliefs. Now look back at your answers to the visualization exercise in Chapter 1. Are your current financial beliefs in conflict with your ultimate life goals? If they are, write them down below.

These are my current financial beliefs that are at odds with my ultimate life goals:

_____

_____

_____

_____

_____

_____

_____

_____

It's okay if you have conflicts. Simply acknowledging them gives you power because now *you* can decide if you need (or want) to make changes to your current beliefs or if you are on the right track and just need to let time take its course. It's important to note that this exercise can also lead you to conclude that your current financial beliefs and ultimate life goals are already in alignment—if so, congratulations. No matter what the conclusion, the key point is that you are now in possession of extremely powerful and important knowledge.

This is serious business. You've just completed a critical step in the process of becoming truly powerful with your money. Getting Financially Naked is all about self-knowledge and self-acceptance. The work you have done in this chapter will serve as the foundation to help you be successful in shaping your dream financial future. This is an exercise you can—and should—do over and over in your life.

If at any point you find yourself somewhere you don't want to be financially, come back and ask yourself this: Are any of my current financial beliefs blocking me from where I want to be?

Time to Get Naked—Together!

Next up, it's time to Get Financially Naked with your honey. Just as your head is full of money histories and current financial beliefs, so too is your mate's. Do you know the key components of your partner's money history? Do you have a solid understanding of your mate's current financial beliefs? Are your financial beliefs and those of your mate compatible? By the time you've finished the next chapter, you will have laid the foundation for Part B of this book where the rubber meets the road in terms of talking money with your honey.

CHAPTER THREE

Do It with Your Partner

I t's not terribly romantic to point this out, but for centuries, marriage was more of an economic than a romantic union. Girl met—or more likely was betrothed to—boy. Girl brought sheep and goats to boy as part of marriage. Boy earned income (or bartered for stuff), and that was pretty much it. Money trumped love. While perhaps not a recipe for marital bliss, it sure seems pretty simple in hindsight.

Oh, how times have changed. We see people marrying early, late, or not at all. We have committed couples who choose not to marry. We have people taking mates of the opposite gender and people taking mates of the same gender. We have people bringing all sorts of things to their relationships, some of which are clearly not as productive as sheep or goats. Couples today find themselves melding assets—and debts—of all sizes and shapes. We have never-married parents. We have divorced parents who bring everything from children and previous spouses to business obligations to their new relationships. Boy meets girl is a simple story of the past.

The More Things Change— the More They Stay the Same

One thing that hasn't changed is that couples, whatever their stripes, generally still don't discuss topics related to money. For all the talk about sex being the last taboo, from what we've seen, that honor clearly goes to money.

Many people still assume their Prince or Princess Charming has it all together, financially speaking. While this book is dedicated to all women, it's important to point out that this dynamic works in the reverse too. Many men tell us they feel as reluctant to probe a potential mate's financial past as they do their sexual past. They tell us it feels intrusive and off limits. Women tell us the same thing, often saying they worry they'll sound like a "gold digger" if they bring up the subject. Interestingly, even those who do bring up the topic tell us they often feel awkward asking questions, as if doing so is a direct attack on the very strength and virility of their partner.

Consider the woman with a graduate degree in business who recently got married only to discover her partner's financial situation was nothing like what she thought. When we asked her why she didn't talk about money with her husband before they were married, she responded, "Well, when we were dating I thought it would be presumptuous to talk about money. Once we were engaged, things got so busy planning for our wedding that next thing you know, it was our wedding day. I had no idea about my partner's financial situation."

Or consider the talented beautician who was swept off her feet by the man who soon became her husband. He was a businessman, so once they were married, it seemed completely natural to her to hand over her paycheck every other week for him to manage. She didn't like dealing with money and since he had a successful business, she figured her Prince Charming knew how to handle money. Unfortunately, after just two years of marriage he walked out on her—emptying their joint bank account the day before, and leaving her with virtually nothing. For this thirty-something hard-working woman, the silver lining was that she learned from the situation and was determined that it would never happen again.

We're not suggesting that women are the only ones to blame for a lack of money discussions in relationships. Far from it.

However, if we ladies are to stand on our own two feet and protect ourselves, we need to learn to be more proactive in raising the topic of money.

Forget Size, What Really Matters Is Financial Compatibility

Once you know what you want to do when it comes to your money, it makes sense to ensure that you are on the same page with your honey. All too often, we hear stories about very smart women (and men) who just "assume" things will work out when it comes to love and money. We've also heard of many instances where people "meant to" discuss the topic, but never got around to it with their 24/7 crazy busy lives.

The bottom line is that financial compatibility is as important as emotional and physical compatibility when it comes to the success of a serious, committed relationship.

As we mentioned earlier, a nationwide survey conducted for *Money Magazine* revealed that 85 percent of respondents note that money causes tension in their marriage. The sad reality is that had money been talked about honestly and openly once the relationship became serious, 85 percent of participants might have reported money caused no (or, at least, less) tension in their marriages. In a different poll conducted by *USA Today*, nearly two-thirds of married couples who responded said they talked very little or not at all about how to combine their finances before the wedding. Left unaddressed, or addressed too late, money issues can fester to the point that, like termites, they literally wreck homes. While the two polls were conducted specifically on married couples, the concepts we are discussing here pertain to anyone in a serious, committed relationship. When it comes to relationship success, communication is essential.

It's Time to Do It with Your Partner

As we've given speeches over the years to countless women, we've heard many stories about how awkward it can be to bring up the topic of money. Here is a sampling of some of the responses women fear or have actually received when they tried to broach the subject:

HEY HONEY—LET'S TALK MONEY . . .
- "Are you thinking about leaving me?"
- "What, don't you trust me?"
- "Why do you want to know how much we have?"
- "That's just not something you need to worry about, I've got it under control."
- "I don't feel like talking about that right now."

We often say that if you are willing to take your clothes off in one way, you should be willing to Get Financially Naked. Specifically, we believe a couple will save much heartache down the road by learning to talk about money in the early stages of their committed relationship. We say "learning to talk" because this isn't a one-time event where each of you asks a couple of questions and then you're done.

As you and your mate transition through life, your financial situation—demands, options, and choices—will evolve. If anything, it will likely get more complex as you collectively take on more responsibilities (two cars, a home, various types of insurance, children and all the costs that go with them, starting a business, etc.) and, hopefully, bring home larger paychecks.

Let's start with understanding your partner's views on money. Just as you laid out your visualization, money history, and current financial beliefs in the past two chapters, it's time to do the same for your partner. If your partner is up for it, you can have him or her walk through the very same exercises you did in the first two chapters. Our experience has been, however, that many mates need to be eased into this conversation gently. So if your mate isn't begging you to download an extra copy of those exercises from *www.GetFinanciallyNaked .com*, you can try the exercise that follows. We suggest you try to have fun with this. Ask your partner to respond verbally to these (yes, add a glass of wine if that helps . . .) and each of you share your responses.

FINANCIAL FOREPLAY—REVVING THINGS UP

- When is the first time you remember money being talked about in your family when you were growing up?
- When growing up, was money ever a source of tension in your household? If so, how would you like it to be different in your future? If not, what tips do you have to make sure that same positive experience repeats in your future?
- When you hear the word "MONEY," what are the first three things that come to mind?
- What are your "money absolutes"—the things you feel in your heart are vital to your financial peace of mind?
- How do you define financial success?

Once you start to talk money with your honey, it can actually be incredibly liberating. Many couples say it takes a huge weight off to know where they each stand when it comes to this often-loaded subject.

Can't We Just Skip This Part?

At this point, you may be getting cold feet. You would not be alone in thinking, "There is *no way* my partner is going to be receptive to this discussion." Or, "Things are going so well in our relationship. What if I upset my partner by bringing up the topic?" If you are getting the urge not to talk money with your mate, we're here to remind you that money is the number one cause of stress in life in general and the number one cause of fights in a relationship. If it's a point of stress in your relationship now, it very likely will be in the future unless you get ahead of it—now. More often than not, this stress comes less from the underlying financial issues themselves, than from avoiding the discussion to begin with or not realizing that you have conflicting goals. We'll say it again and again: money issues are a huge contributor to the 50 percent divorce rate in this country. Our point isn't to scare or depress you, but rather to say that as unsexy as it is to discuss money, it's *much more* sexy and *far less painful* than having a relationship end because of money.

The Upside of Talking Money with Your Honey

The way in which your partner responds to your attempts to bring up this vital subject will speak volumes about whether you've got the right partner. If your partner is receptive, reluctant, embarrassed, shy, or angry, it's in your best interest to contemplate and digest that response. Your partner should at least be a little receptive initially. That's all you need, just a small opening. If you get that, you (both) are on the right path and ready to move on to the next section of this book. If you don't get an opening, you'll want to take a step back and re-evaluate. Perhaps your partner has trust or communication issues that you can work on together—or with professional help.

Knowledge Is Power—Now Act on It

In Parts B and C of this book, we'll give you the practical "how to's" to take this dialogue to the next level. We'll kick it off in Chapter 4 with a financial compatibility quiz for you and your mate. This will help you both start to understand how you approach money matters on a practical basis. Chapter 4 sets the foundation for the remainder of the book by starting the critical dialogue that will ultimately bring you and your mate closer by creating an honest and open mutual vision for your financial future.

PART B

TALKING MONEY WITH YOUR HONEY

CHAPTER FOUR

How Financially Compatible Are You?

When Valentine's Day rolls around, one of the most popular talks we have been asked to give on TV and radio shows is called "Are You Dating a Deadbeat?" It's a series of five questions designed to help women (and men) make sure that their fluttering hearts are caused by love and not palpitations from financial fears about their mate. One of the key messages of this book is that until you dare to Get Financially Naked, you don't really know if your partner's outer public image is an accurate reflection of his or her inner financial reality.

While the following Valentine's Day Q&A definitely has an infusion of humor to lighten things up, the stark reality is that every single time we give these five tips, we hear yet another story about someone who thought their mate had it together financially, but sadly did not. The list below will get you thinking and provide some examples of how your honey might be living beyond his/her means.

HAPPY VALENTINE'S DAY — ARE YOU DATING A DEADBEAT?

DOES YOUR SWEETIE ALWAYS INSIST ON PICKING UP THE CHECK AT A BIG DINNER AND/OR THROW DOWN HIS OR HER CREDIT CARD WITHOUT EVEN LOOKING AT THE BILL? While this could be a sign of innate generosity, it could also be a red flag for someone who is trying to show off and is doing so by living beyond his or her means, thanks to the "friendly" help of credit cards.

DOES YOUR SWEETIE LEASE HIS OR HER CAR? Think about it, what's the sales pitch for leasing? It's, "Hey, you can get more car for less money than if you buy outright!" When it comes to your money, if it sounds too good to be true, it usually is. While there are a handful of situations where leasing can make sense, more often than not it is a red financial flag that someone may be living beyond their means.

DOES YOUR SWEETIE HAVE A LARGE BUT SPARSELY FURNISHED APARTMENT/HOME? While it's possible that your sweetie is just waiting for his or her personal design sensibility to present itself . . . more likely than not it's a sign that they've got a case of what's called down in Texas "Big Hat, No Cattle."

DOES YOUR SWEETIE AVOID ANSWERING CALLS ON HIS OR HER PHONE? It's possible that it's just mom checking in to see how the day is going . . . but then again, it's also possible that it's bill collectors calling to find out when your sweetie is going to make good on that car payment, mortgage, credit card, or other outstanding debts.

DOES YOUR SWEETIE ASK YOU TO CO-SIGN OR BUY THINGS IN YOUR NAME, PROMISING TO PAY YOU BACK? Why would a financially responsible person ever ask their significant other to do this? If something smells fishy to you, it's likely not the dinner you cooked last night.

The truth is that millions of Americans, of both genders, need help understanding how to approach the subject of money. In the last chapter, we began with some very basic "financial foreplay." Our intent was simply for you and your mate to *start* talking about personal finance. By design, we didn't raise any truly loaded questions. Our goal was for both you and your partner to begin to think about the role money played in your life when you were growing up—and what that has meant, broadly speaking, for how you relate to money today. We wanted you and your mate to see that you've both had interactions with money for years and the sum total of all those seemingly small experiences have collectively formed your view and your behavior regarding money today.

In this chapter, we're going to ask you and your mate to rip those clothes off and really start to Get Financially Naked.

Where the Rubber Meets the Road

As we've traveled the country for the past few years, we always tell people that the first step in this process is to understand what each of you **Owns**, what each of you **Owes**, what you **Earn**, and what your **Credit Score** is. For most people, what you own, owe, and earn are straightforward concepts, while credit scores are not always as widely understood. In case you are wondering, your credit score is a three-digit number that summarizes how financially responsible you've been to date. We all have one, and you should know what yours is. Many people don't realize this, but your credit score is used for all sorts of things like determining how much you'd pay for a home or car loan, whether a landlord will rent to you, what kinds of rates insurance companies will charge you, and even if an employer is willing to hire you. That's why it's such an important number. Taken together, these four pieces of information (what you

own, owe, earn, and your credit score) will form the foundation of your financial intimacy with each other.

We are talking about Getting Financially Naked when you
are in a serious and committed relationship. The most common
question we get when we give this advice is, "What does a serious
committed relationship really mean and when exactly do we Get
Financially Naked?" We define a serious committed relationship
as one where you trust the person you are with and you can see
yourself with this person for the long term. Exactly when that
moment happens in your relationship will be highly personal.
We know people who've felt it on the second date and others
who didn't feel it until they were in the second year of dating.

The key is that once you get the gut feeling telling you
that this is "The One," it's time to start Getting Financially
Naked.

If you are not in a serious relationship today, are just dating
around, or are not even dating at all, please continue reading.
Having a solid understanding of this process before Cupid's
arrow hits will be critical to helping you stand on your own two
feet and live your life from a position of financial strength when
that special person arrives. You need to know now what to do
when love strikes, because the odds are high that when you
meet the one, reading a book on personal finance is not going

to be high up on your list of to-dos. Before we get into the nuts and bolts, however, let's address three of the most common questions that we get whenever we bring up this subject.

THREE COMMON QUESTIONS ABOUT GETTING FINANCIALLY NAKED

WHEN IS IT OKAY TO BRING UP MONEY WITH MY MATE? IS IT OKAY TO DO IT WHEN WE ARE JUST DATING? We believe the earlier the better. That said, our intention is NOT to cause your sweetie to freak out on a first date by bringing up the subject of the thousands of dollars of credit card or student loan debt that you (or McDreamy) are hoping to pay off. Our point is simply that once you can see yourself getting serious with your potential mate, we believe it's time to start talking about money. As to the exact timing, again, it really is up to the unique nature of your particular relationship. For instance, if you are wondering how your mate can afford the fancy Vegas vacations and high-priced meals on a teacher's salary, it's reasonable to bring up money early on. Or if you have some financial hiccups of your own, we believe it's important to come clean earlier rather than later. We've heard of all too many seemingly promising relationships that end when, after an extended period of dating, one partner discovers the other is deep in debt. Typically, this issue is not so much the debt, as the fact that it was not discussed early on. When you start to Get Financially Naked, you'll learn a lot about your financial compatibility simply by seeing how your honey responds to your bringing up the topic of money.

WHAT IF I KNOW MY PARTNER IS NOT RECEPTIVE—OR I FIND OUT DURING THE CONVERSATION THAT MY PARTNER IS NOT RECEPTIVE—TO TALKING ABOUT THE TOPIC OF MONEY? Just because you get an initial cold shoulder doesn't mean you two are doomed in the financial harmony department. Our recommendation is to tee up the conversation by talking about *your* views on money, and seeing if you can ease in with the Financial Foreplay questions from Chapter 3. The key is this: Don't give up and be persistent. Your mate's reluctance to discuss money could simply be a sign of painful, but resolvable, issues in their money history (recall the exercise you did in Chapter 2 about your money history and what you learned about yourself). A cold shoulder does not mean it is okay to just ignore the conversation about money. It means there are some underlying issues that, if explored, may actually bring you closer—emotionally and financially.

As you approach the topic of money with your honey, if your partner is reluctant to talk about money, you'll want to be very sensitive to how you respond to anything that does bubble up. Money is a hot button for many people. When your partner does begin to open up, it is essential that you listen and be supportive to whatever is said. There will be plenty of time down the road to discuss areas of disagreement or places where compromise are needed.

MY PARTNER IS WONDERFUL, LOVING, AND VERY GENEROUS TOWARD ME. HOWEVER, I'M WORRIED BECAUSE THE MATH JUST DOESN'T SEEM TO ADD UP. WHEN I LOOK AT WHAT MY MATE DOES FOR A LIVING, IT DOESN'T APPEAR TO BE THE TYPE OF CAREER WITH THE SALARY LEVEL NECESSARY TO PAY FOR THE KIND OF LIFESTYLE MY PARTNER LEADS. HOW DO I BRING THIS UP? The harsh and sad truth is that literally millions of Americans, at all ranges of the income spectrum, live beyond their means. They bridge the gap between their income and their expenses by running up hefty balances on their credit cards or taking equity out of their home. If this is how your mate is funding his or her lifestyle, you owe it to each other and the integrity of your relationship to know about it. Maintaining a lifestyle beyond your reach using credit is not sustainable and typically ends up resulting in severe financial distress—not to mention the possibility of being hounded by bill collectors or ending up in foreclosure. One way or another you two will end up discussing your finances. Your goal is to do so before it torpedoes your relationship.

You know it's time to Get Financially Naked when . . .

Here are some classic signs: Your partner wants to spend more and you are borrowing money from your family to support this lifestyle. You look at how your partner's family lives and it doesn't seem to add up, which may be a red flag that your partner has been trained to live beyond his or her means. You start wondering about your household financial facts and you encounter resistance. For example, your partner says everything will be okay and there's no need to worry about it. There are many more signs, but here are three that indicate it's time to make talking money with your mate a top priority.

Time to Start Peeling Back the Layers

Before stripping down to your financial bare bones (by disclosing what you own, what you owe, what you earn, and your credit score), we're going to ask you and your partner to take a "Financial Compatibility" quiz. There are thirty Yes / No questions for each of you to answer. It's a short exercise that should take less than ten minutes to complete. Once you've both completed the quiz, we'll ask you to share and compare your answers.

Some of you may be wondering—how scientific is this quiz? The short answer is: it's not. It's a simple exercise designed to help the two of you understand how you both approach money. There is no right answer or best score. The quiz has three sections (Interest, Knowledge, and Behavior) with ten questions about money in each. There's no judgment here. Any response is a good response because it reveals how you truly feel. All we ask is that you are honest with yourself and your mate in responding to these questions. If you're feeling at all apprehensive or doubtful about the usefulness of this quiz, check out the following list. We've summarized some of the reasons people don't like to talk about money with their mate, as well as how they feel *after* they take the plunge and do so.

COMMON REASONS FOR STAYING QUIET

- "We're so busy planning for the wedding—I'm stressed enough as it is."
- "Work is crazy—who has the time?"
- "We're just dating—I don't want to screw it up or scare my honey off."
- "We just had our first child—are you insane, if I have free time I'm going to sleep!"
- "If I wanted to feel nauseated, I'd eat raw liver."

COMMON RESPONSES AFTER OPENING UP

- "Wow, I feel lighter, it's like this huge weight has been lifted off my shoulders."
- "Amazing, I feel closer to my mate than I ever have. It's like we're really in this together now."
- "Huge stress relief—we still don't have all the answers but now I get where my honey is coming from, and I feel heard in return."

- "It's like after you've just weeded out your closet, order is restored."
- "For me it was like financial Metamucil. You know that feeling when you are cleansed and relieved? That's what this quiz did for me."

Hopefully, this collection of honest feedback has made you realize that you are not alone. Nearly any feeling you've ever had about money, someone else has had at some point or another—we're all in this together. So let's get started with the quiz so you and your mate can finally move toward your dream financial life.

Important note: If you are not in a committed relationship right now, go ahead and fill out this quiz in the context of your own personal financial situation. You'll learn a lot about yourself. If you are in a committed relationship, you'll still want to fill out the quiz on your own (and have your partner do it separately as well). However, you'll want your answers to be in the context of your household. For instance, you may know how much of *your* income you are saving for retirement, but for purposes of this questionnaire you'll want to answer the question for your household, i.e., do you know how much both you and your mate are saving relative to your combined incomes, etc. (You can download additional copies of this quiz at *www.GetFinanciallyNaked.com*.)

THE "GET FINANCIALLY NAKED" COMPATIBILITY QUIZ

KNOWLEDGE	Yes	No
1. You know how much money you need to cover your regular monthly expenses.		
2. You know how much money you need for your personal three to six month emergency fund.		
3. You know how much you should aim to save for retirement as a percentage of your income.		
4. You know where all of your money is stored today (all bank accounts and other financial accounts including retirement accounts).		
5. You know how much money you owe for all your debts, and the interest rates you are being charged on each.		
6. You understand basic concepts regarding how to invest your money.		
7. You know how much risk you're willing to take with your investments.		
8. You know what your top five financial goals are.		
9. You know the key types of insurance you need to protect your loved ones and assets.		
10. You know where your essential documents are stored.		

INTEREST	Yes	No
1. You enjoy reading financial books, magazines, newsletters, or blogs.		
2. You enjoy watching financial TV shows or listening to radio programs.		
3. You enjoy talking about financial matters.		
4. You often think about your personal financial situation and how to improve it.		
5. You often think about whether you are on track to meet your retirement and other big financial goals.		
6. You are interested in the financial details of your day-to-day life.		
7. You believe money issues need to be addressed today, rather than letting them resolve themselves over time.		
8. You prioritize having financial security and stability in your life.		
9. You spend time thinking about protecting your assets.		
10. You believe having money leads to good outcomes.		

BEHAVIOR	Yes	No
1. You always pay your bills on time.		
2. You track your progress in terms of meeting your financial goals.		
3. You regularly look at your bank or other financial account balances.		
4. You are on track to save 10 percent or more of your before-tax income for retirement (if not today, you are committed to over time).		

BEHAVIOR—*continued*	Yes	No
5. You are paying off debt in a planned, systematic way, i.e., starting with the highest interest rate first.		
6. You regularly check your credit reports to make sure there are no errors (or that identity theft has not occurred) and you know what your credit score is.		
7. Any money that you invest in individual stocks (not mutual funds) is money that you can afford to lose.		
8. You have a will or living trust and an appropriate loved one or trustee also has a copy.		
9. You have enough insurance to cover your needs, including sufficient life insurance if you have kids.		
10. You ask financial professionals for help when you need it.		

When you are done, simply go through each section and add up the number of times you answered "yes" to a question, and then fill in the following chart.

GET FINANCIALLY NAKED FINANCIAL COMPATIBILITY QUIZ RESULTS
Total the Number of Yes Responses per Section

	Your Results	**Your Partner's Results**
Knowledge	_____/ 10	_____/ 10
Interest	_____/ 10	_____/ 10
Behavior	_____/ 10	_____/ 10

Okay, now it's time to debrief. Here are some questions to kick it off:

- Which section did you have the most number of "yes" responses to? The fewest?
- Were you surprised by your answers? What did you learn about yourself?
- Which area did your mate have the most "yes" responses to? The fewest?
- Were the results for your partner what you would have expected?
- Are there any subject areas you think you two should talk more about?

SAMPLE REACTIONS AFTER DOING THE QUIZ

- "Whew . . . no surprises. This quiz validated how we've been handling our money and reaffirmed our game plan."
- "Eye-opening . . . I realized both of us have no idea how much we should be saving for retirement. We are saving, but this made me realize I have no idea if we are doing enough."
- "I realized my Prince Charming isn't as sharp with money as I thought. He's always watching all these financial shows on TV so I thought he had it together, but his behavior score showed me he's not walking the walk."
- "Empowering. This quiz made me realize that while our individual accounts are fine, we really aren't working together on our joint saving and investing goals."

- "Liberating . . . my sweetie got so excited that I wanted to talk about money. He said he's been wanting to talk to me about our spending for a while but wasn't sure how to bring it up without my freaking out or feeling like he wasn't a good provider."

Taking It to the Next Level

You now have some intimate knowledge about each other's financial tendencies. This is where we dial it up one more notch.

We want you to make a list of what you own, what you owe, what you earn, and your credit scores.

Note: Whether you fill out this list based on your individual data or based on your combined data will depend upon the specific nature of your relationship at this time. For instance, if you are contemplating moving in together or you are married and per a prenuptial have separate finances, do these lists separately. If you are already married or have otherwise merged your assets, do this list on a combined basis.

So here you go, fill out the form that follows—you're about to Get Financially Naked. (Download extra forms at *www.Get*

FinanciallyNaked.com if you and your honey want to fill this
out separately.)

YOUR GET FINANCIALLY NAKED STATEMENT

What you Own	Current Dollar Value
Home	
Car	
Employer-sponsored retirement accounts, such as a 401(k) plan	
Individual Retirement Accounts (IRAs)	
Checking accounts	
Savings accounts	
Taxable brokerage accounts	
Other	
TOTAL OWNED	

What you Owe	Current Dollar Value
Mortgage	
Home equity loan	
Car loan	
Student loans	
Credit card debt	
Any other debt(s)	
TOTAL OWED	

The difference between what you *own* and what you *owe* is your net worth. Calculate your current net worth here:

Current Net Worth (Total Owned - Total Owed)	

What You Earn	Dollar Value
Expected income this year	
Expected income next year	

Note: There are various ways you can share your earning history. One is just by filling out this worksheet or by sharing a recent pay stub. If you really want to dial it up, you could exchange tax returns for the past few years. How you do it is up to you, but the important thing is to be honest with each other. If you are in a committed relationship, your incomes should not be a secret from each other.

Your FICO Credit Score from One of the Three Big Credit Bureaus

You can get your FICO credit score at *www.MyFico.com*. As of this writing, it will cost you approximately $15 to purchase one of your credit scores. There are three different credit bureaus—Equifax, Experian, and TransUnion—that will calculate and sell you your FICO credit score. These three firms use slightly different computations to arrive at your score. For the purposes of this exercise, however, it does not matter which of the three credit bureaus you select. Your goal simply is to get a sense of the current state of your credit. FICO scores range from 300 to 850—and higher is better.

Your Credit Score(s)	
Yours	
Your Honey's	

Extra Credit—Your Credit Reports

You can go to *www.AnnualCreditReport.com* and get your credit reports from each of the three major credit bureaus at no cost once a year. (Note: There are many imposter sites. You want to use *www.AnnualCreditReport.com*, as it was set up specifically in response to government legislation designed to help consumers.) If you are interested in learning more about credit scores and credit reports, we recommend reading our first book, *On My Own Two Feet*. For now, just keep in mind that your credit score is a three-digit number that summarizes how financially responsible you are and it is based on information that is stored in these credit reports.

The reason you are getting these reports (for you and your mate) is to make sure you each can see, as reported by an outside party, what is on your financial record.

The first time you check your reports, we recommend that you order all three at once. Remember, they are free once a year. Then starting the following year, order one every four months so you can keep a constant watch on your report (mark your calendar so you remember). This is vital because the information used on these reports is used to calculate your credit score.

Now, set the mood—this may require candles, jazz, a beverage of choice, whatever you two need—and sit down together to collect and review this information. Collecting all this information is a bit tedious, but trust us, it's worth it.

Compatibility Is Key, Now You Can Move Forward—Together

This information will set the foundation for the rest of this book. Having this information is the financial equivalent of establishing a rock solid foundation under your house. This step makes the magic possible. The truth is that once you can see where you are starting from, you can make the choices that will bring you closer to that life that makes your heart sing—closer to that vision you laid out for yourself back in Chapter 1. This is where it all begins . . . with Getting Financially Naked and knowing what you own, what you owe, what you earn, and what your credit score is. Congratulations. You've taken one giant leap toward owning your finances and owning your life.

CHAPTER FIVE

The Five Power Steps to Financial Success

There is an old Indian parable about a hard working, cash-strapped villager whose prized possession, his icebox (what we'd call a refrigerator today), broke down. The villager sent a message to the repairman with the best reputation around to come fix it. The repairman arrived early the next morning and sat down in front of the icebox. Every now and then, he'd open the door or tilt it over to look on the underside. The villager paced back and forth, wondering what the heck was going on. Where was the action, the sweat, the intricate and detailed work?

Finally, hours later, the repairman pulled out a hammer and hit the icebox once. It started working immediately. The repairman turned to the villager and said, that will be 500 rupees. At this point, the villager totally lost it. "Are you out of your mind—you want to charge me 500 rupees for swinging a hammer one time? I could have done that myself!" The repairman smiled kindly, and replied gently, "Actually, sir, I am only charging you 1 rupee for the hammer hit. I'm charging you 499 rupees to decide what spot required the hit." What does this story have to do with your personal finances? Everything.

> The personal finance landscape has gotten so complicated these days that it's easy to confuse activity with progress.

In the aforementioned tale, the villager was surprised to find out that focusing on one critical action could totally turn a situation around. The same goes for our personal finances. Many of us get so overwhelmed with the ability of technology to enable us to go in fifty directions at once that we forget to focus on what is really important to our bottom lines. Take Paul and Shirlee for example. Paul, to put it mildly, is a bit intense. He has spreadsheets galore set up to track everything from how much they pay per ounce for peanut butter to how many minutes they end up losing each month on their fixed rate cell phone plan. He drags Shirlee through so many mundane details that she hates talking with him about anything related to their personal finances. After taking our advice, however, Shirlee realized they were wasting a lot of energy. When she realized that it's the big stuff that truly matters, and that's what their joint financial conversations really needed to focus on, it was a huge relief. That type of conversation felt totally manageable to her. As we see in this example, the confusion between "activity and progress" can often lead to a huge amount of tension between couples when it comes to their money.

To find financial harmony, you and your mate need to get on the same page about the handful of financial decisions that really drive lasting financial success. We call these the Five Power Steps to Financial Success. As you talk through these powerful steps, remember this:

> With a commitment to communication, honesty, and perhaps a dash of compromise, you can achieve financial peace of mind as a couple.

Such peace of mind will likely bring you two closer and allow you to feel confident that your shared future is on solid financial ground. If you are single today, implementing these five power steps in your current financial life will go a long way toward positioning you to achieve financial harmony when you do couple up.

So what are these steps? They are the decisions you make surrounding five of your largest lifetime expenses.

FIVE KEY LIFETIME EXPENSES

1. Your Home
2. Your Car
3. Your Retirement
4. Your Kids (including education)
5. Your (extended) Family Obligations

The decisions you make in these five areas typically consume the lion's share of your budget over the course of your life. That's why they are so important for you and your mate to discuss. The good news here, and the point of the opening story, is that to make good choices you don't have to engage in a lot of frantic activity. Making one or two smart, accurate decisions about the key areas of your financial life is often all that is required to put you on solid financial footing. In fact, more often than not the best financial decisions are the ones you make when you remind yourself to keep it simple. Plan and spend wisely in the five areas we've listed and you've just turbocharged your financial future without adding a lot of complexity to your life.

In this chapter, we will give you a basic framework to use in thinking about the first three of these five vital lifestyle decisions: your home, car, and funding your retirement. In the next chapter, we'll talk about your children—which for many people is their next largest source of spending after their home—and other family obligations. Addressing each of these key areas as early on in your relationship as possible will go a long way toward ensuring financial and emotional harmony in your relationship and your budget.

Power Step #1: Ask Yourself, "How Much Home Can We *Really* Afford?"

Millions of Americans have found themselves in the unfortunate situation of biting off more house than they can chew. Nancy and Ned are classic examples. Ever since Nancy and Ned got married three years ago, they have heard the same question over and over from friends and family: "Why are you still renting? Don't you know that's just throwing money down the drain? Don't you know you are losing out on a huge tax deduction?" It was the tax deduction—and their friends and family's constant nagging—that put them over the edge. They felt stupid for not taking advantage of it. So Nancy and Ned bought a home in December 2006. That was—as they would later find out—right at the peak of the housing market. Fast forward a couple of years and Nancy got her dream job— in another state. They had to sell quickly during the housing downturn, and ended up owing the bank more than they got for the sale of the house. Chasing after a tax deduction

—which, ironically, they never got because they were so busy during tax season they opted for the standard deduction rather than go through the hassle of itemizing—left them hostage to their house.

Are You Really Getting That Tax Deduction?

Many people don't realize that, under current tax laws, mortgage interest isn't automatically deductible. You have to itemize your deductions to receive it and experts have concluded that a full two-thirds of Americans take the standard deduction on their income taxes. Make sure you buy your home for the right reasons and not for the primary purpose of a tax deduction.

For decades, home ownership has been synonymous with the American Dream. When you couple up, it's not uncommon for friends and family to start asking you, as they did Nancy and Ned, "So when are you buying a place?" As a result, millions of us aspire to be homeowners. The key is to do it in a way that makes your home your haven, not a financial ball and chain. In recent years, record numbers of American mortgages are either delinquent or in foreclosure. As millions of hardworking American families have come to find out, "qualify" does not mean the same thing as "afford." At the risk of stating the obvious, this has led to huge tensions in many American households of late. The good news is that you and your partner can help protect yourselves by employing some keep-it-simple rules of thumb and engaging in straightforward communication (with a side helping of compromise)

Most people can comfortably afford a home that is up to *three times* their annual household income.*

Note: This rule of thumb assumes interest rates in the 5 to 6 percent range. If interest rates ever soar up to 10 percent, the rule of thumb would drop to two times your income.

Let's take Amy and Jack as an example. Their combined household income is $60,000. That means they can comfortably afford a home that costs $180,000. The only way Amy and Jack can comfortably afford more house than this would be if they expected a dramatic—and sustained—rise in their household income over the coming years *or* if they would be willing to significantly cut back on how much they will spend in other areas of their life. The rationale behind this rule of thumb has to do with your budget. Many people think budgets are constraining or about deprivation.

Used correctly, a budget is actually a liberating and empowering tool that lets you track the flow of money in and out of your life.

Given that housing is such a major expense for most people, it's all the more important to know how it fits into that outflow of money.

Think of your gross income as a pie totaling 100 percent (where gross income is just a fancy way of saying your income *before taxes*).

YOUR GROSS INCOME

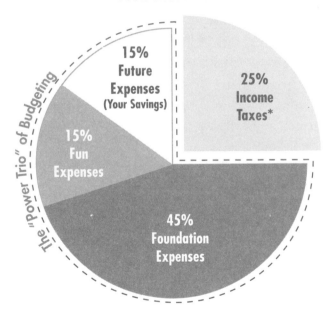

*This sample pie assumes a 25% effective income tax rate. If your taxes are more than 25%, you will have less than 75% left over to spend.

Once taxes are paid, what is left over is money that you will spend on your foundation expenses (the must haves), your fun expenses (the nice to haves), and your future expenses (saving for your future—the biggest chunk of which is for your retirement). If you spend three times your income on a home, your all-in housing costs will be about 30 percent of your gross income. As you can see from the previous graphic, that's the majority of your foundation expenses.

Remember, when you buy a house the cost of home ownership is not just limited to your monthly mortgage payment. It also includes your property taxes, insurance, utilities, maintenance, and upkeep. If you stretch much beyond the three times your household income rule of thumb for the purchase price of your home, you will likely have to make some tough tradeoffs. Why? Because once you factor in your mortgage payment plus all those other related housing costs, you won't have much left for the rest of your essential foundation expenses such as your car, food, insurance, child care, etc. Recall from the gross income pie that most people have roughly 45 percent to spend on *all* of their foundation expenses.

Our point here is to arm you and your partner with the financial facts so you can have an open, honest conversation where you make the best choices to fit your life. You may decide to spend a little more than you can comfortably afford right now in hopes that your income will catch up with you down the road. But if you do, we want you to make sure you understand the tradeoffs and what you are getting into. While your decision will be highly personal, one universal point is that you will dramatically increase your odds of monetary and relationship bliss if you are open-eyed about the financial impact.

Plan and Prioritize *Together*

If, after careful thought, you both decide to buy your dream house right now, you may both choose to temporarily limit other areas of spending or saving. For example, you could temporarily limit your contributions to your respective retirement plans at work (making sure you always contribute to the point of your employer's match), tucking the rest of your savings away for a 20 percent down payment. Alternatively, you both may decide to pay just the minimum on your student loans, if the interest rate is reasonable, until you've saved up for the 20 percent down payment. There are lots of options, just make sure to do your research and think through the pros and cons.

For the vast majority of couples, the only way to achieve lasting financial harmony will be to understand where each other is coming from with regards to all major financial decisions—and then to find a compromise that meets everyone's needs.

HOME BUYING RULES OF THUMB

1. **Build up a 20 percent down payment before you buy your home.** As many people learned during the painful 2008–2009 housing crisis, home prices don't always go up. A 20 percent down payment helps give you some cushion in case you have to sell your home in a hurry

(think about Nancy and Ned: you finally get that dream job—but it's in another state). When you buy a home, you run the risk that the price of the home may go down. If that happens when it comes time to sell, you'll really want that 20 percent cushion so you don't end up owing the bank more than you get for the sale of your home.

2. **Don't buy unless you know you will live in your home for at least five years.** The costs associated with buying and selling a home can easily add up to 10 percent of a home's value. By living in your home for at least five years, you increase the odds that when you do sell, your house will have appreciated enough to offset these costs (and hopefully even leave you with a profit).

3. **Consider the oldie but goodie—the thirty-year fixed rate mortgage.** When it comes to mortgages, we believe simple is best. Unless you have a solid understanding of what you are getting into with a "fancy" mortgage, such as an adjustable rate mortgage or interest-only mortgage, we believe the good old-fashioned thirty-year (or fifteen-year) fixed rate mortgage is the way to go.

HOUSING QUESTIONS TO DISCUSS WITH YOUR MATE
- Do we want to buy a home and if so, when would we ideally like to do it?
- Are we buying a home that we both feel good about and for the right reasons?
- What's our financial plan to get there?

Power Step #2: Ask Yourself, "How Much Car Can We Comfortably Afford?"

Who hasn't gone to the car dealership and, intoxicated by that new-car smell, thought just for a nanosecond, "I would eat Spam and ramen noodles for the rest of my life if only I could have *this* car?" Many Americans have a love affair with their cars, and this can be costly to their financial health. It's worth spending some quality time thinking about what a car means to both you and your mate. Are either of you spending more than you can comfortably afford on your wheels? If so, is the implicit tradeoff worth it? Note, we say *implicit* because money spent on a car is money that isn't being spent or saved elsewhere. If one of you is a genuine auto buff, it may be worth the money to buy a little more car—and make cutbacks elsewhere. The key is to be informed and deliberate about the decisions you make together.

Just as with a house, remember that the all-in cost of a car includes much more than just your monthly payment. It also includes car insurance, gas, parking and/or tolls, maintenance, and upkeep. To keep your car from driving you to the poorhouse, you'll want to aim to keep your total transportation costs to 10 percent or less of your gross income. What's the best way to do this? Following is a simple rule of thumb.

To have a balanced budget, aim to keep the *total* purchase price of your car(s) to 30 percent *or less* of your total annual (before-tax) household income.

Exhaust All Your Car Options

As you venture out to buy a car, to get more bang for your buck, consider the value in a certified pre-owned car. You can get them through dealerships or retailers like *www.CarMax.com*. If you do buy a new car, we encourage you to own it for five-plus years to get your money's worth. Remember, the minute you drive a new car off the showroom lot, it starts losing value and the average car loses half its value in three years — so you want to keep that new car around for a good long while.

The key takeaway from this section is that it's important to talk with your mate about what a car means to each of you. Are you on the same page? Does one of you see it simply as transportation from point A to point B, while the other sees it as an image statement? Many couples think differently when it comes to cars but that's okay, you just need to plan and budget accordingly. Use the gross income pie on page 82 to talk with your mate about the compromises each of you is willing to make.

CAR QUESTIONS TO DISCUSS WITH YOUR MATE

- What does a car mean to each of us?
- What car(s) make sense for our household at this point in time?
- How would we use any savings from going with a cheaper car?

Power Step #3: Ask Yourself, "Will We Ever Be Able to Retire?"

The economic downturn of 2008–2009 swallowed the nest eggs of many a baby boomer. As such, a new generation of investors is realizing that retirement planning is a critical part of maintaining solid emotional and financial health. When it comes to fully funding an enjoyable retirement, "the number," or the total amount you need to have saved to afford the retirement of your dreams, can take your breath away.

To meet your retirement goals, strive to set aside at least 10 percent of your gross (i.e., before-tax) income every year . . . and invest that money wisely.

Note: The gross income pie example referenced on page 82 identified a total savings goal of 15 percent. That 15 percent includes 10 percent for retirement plus 5 percent for nearer-term expenses such as down payments on a home or car, weddings, college savings for your kids, and so on. We'll talk more about saving in Chapter 7.

The goal of saving at least 10 percent of your gross income for retirement, and assuming you invest wisely, is to maintain your current standard of living in your golden years. This is a very rough rule of thumb and you need to look closely at your personal situation to decide what's right for you. When it comes to retirement, many couples have different expectations or simply do not discuss and plan for it at all.

Consciously or unconsciously, many couples hope that things will simply work out, and the money will be there when needed. This is sort of like hoping you can fit into your prom dress thirty years later without paying any attention to what you eat or how you exercise during the years in between. Unfortunately, the harsh reality for many couples is that they will end up working longer or existing on a much lower standard of living in retirement than they had anticipated.

Discussing retirement—even if it feels a long way off—is a critical financial step, especially for women.

This is because women live longer, spend more time out of the work force raising kids or tending to aging parents, and unfortunately still earn less than men on average. As such, over two-thirds of women over the age of sixty-five are relying on meager Social Security payments as their primary source of income. This means they are quite literally choosing between food and essential medicine. Against this backdrop, it is vital that you and your honey talk about your retirement years. If you feel you need help with retirement planning, we suggest seeking professional counsel, as a comprehensive discussion of retirement is beyond the scope of this short book. And while we recognize that there are many options for getting financial advice, these three are our favorites.

1. Speaking with large, stable financial institutions such as Charles Schwab, Fidelity, and Vanguard that offer a variety of reasonably priced, flexible investment options (research their offering on their respective websites: *www .Schwab.com*, *www.Fidelity.com*, and *www.Vanguard.com*)
2. Seeking the help of an hourly fee-only certified financial planner (you can find one through organizations such as *www.Napfa.org* or *www.GarrettPlanningNetwork.com*)
3. Utilizing the services of a financial planner who charges a set percentage of your assets under management (as opposed to a commission) so your incentives are aligned

To elaborate, let's consider Ria and Lester. They are an example of a couple who benefited from a visit with a financial planner. They have a combined income of $60,000 a year. They meant to save for retirement, but life kept getting in the way. They had heard it was good to save at least 10 percent for retirement, but that percentage didn't really mean anything to them. When they finally sat down with a financial planner to talk about their retirement goals, they realized they'd need more than $1 million in retirement savings to achieve their lifestyle goals. Reality finally sunk in like a ton of bricks. *Now* was the time to start saving for their golden years, because otherwise they'd both be working until their last breaths.

RETIREMENT QUESTIONS TO DISCUSS WITH YOUR MATE

- When do we want to retire?
- Have we started saving for retirement yet?
- How are our retirement savings invested?

If you can tough it out and put these issues on the table, you will likely be amazed to see the positive long run effects on your relationship. It's important to remember that you don't have to discuss everything at once, and the decisions you make do not have to be permanent. For instance, there may be periods in your life when the tradeoffs of having a fancier car are worth it to you—and other periods when they are not. The key for you and the health of your relationship is that you are making these critical decisions in an informed way—together.

A key take-away from this chapter is the following: For most people, the money spent in these three areas will eat up more than 50 percent of their income pie. That's why it's essential to focus on these topics. In the next chapter, we will talk about the other two big areas that can have a dramatic impact on your wallet over the course of your life—kids and extended family members.

CHAPTER SIX

For Better or for Worse . . . You Get the Family Too

As much as we'd all love it if our extended families were like the Brady Bunch—one big happy mishmash of upbeat familial love—it doesn't always turn out that way. Even the closest, warmest, most jovial of families can hit one of life's speed bumps from time to time.

The stark reality is that while many couples will choose to create a family of their own together, each partner already comes to the relationship with their own family background—for better or for worse. Yet our society tends to shy away from talking openly and honestly about the various financial issues that can arise from the creation of and care for a family. There is an arc to human life from birth to adolescence, to adulthood to death. To say it bluntly—every step of the way there are financial issues to deal with. This chapter is dedicated to the remaining two of the Five Power Steps to Financial Success that we outlined in Chapter 5.

Power Step #4: Ask Yourself, "The Stork Has Arrived, Are We Financially Prepared?"

If you decide to have children, those bundles of love will most likely be the biggest source of expenditures for you after your home. Without a doubt, kids are wonderful and all but the most cold-hearted would say the expense is worth it. As we write this book, Sharon has just given birth to her second child. So let us be crystal clear—we're all for having kids. Our point is simply this:

When you bring a child into this world, there are financial consequences, and you and your partner owe it to your family to plan for those responsibilities.

Now, you may say that's all well and good, but not everyone gets to plan a family. Sometimes you are trying for one child and you end up with two—or more! Sometimes you are not even trying at all and you just get surprised. Life happens, and sometimes you have no choice but to just roll with it. Regardless of how your family was started, once you have kids, you owe it to your family to think about the financial impact. Recall that time and again money is cited as a top source of fights in marriage and divorce. As much as it is a blessing to be a parent, there are times when the financial stress of it can be what pushes you over the edge.

Once the initial euphoria of the arrival of a new family member wears off, it's not uncommon for another feeling to arrive—shock and awe. We're talking about the cost of things like diapers (which can run over $30 a box and get run through faster than a pitcher of ice-cold lemonade on a hot summer day). Or what about a crib? These days the most basic models can cost you hundreds of dollars. Then there's baby food, clothes, car seats, not to mention the stuff you never even knew existed, but you now *need* to have. As one mom put it, "I never thought I'd be buying a baby wipe warmer so my little one's bottom has warm wipes to soothe him. I never thought we'd have more clothes for our newborn than for ourselves because our bundle of love spits up so many times a day that we change his clothes more in a day than we do ours in a week!" And no discussion of children is complete without bringing up the question: what about child care? We've heard countless stories of parents who find that their salary barely covers the child care costs after taxes.

DO YOU KNOW HOW MUCH IT COSTS THE AVERAGE FAMILY TO RAISE A CHILD?

Take a guess:
- $50,000
- $100,000
- $150,000
- over $150,000

If you guessed over $150,000, you are correct.

The U.S. Department of Agriculture currently estimates it costs the average middle class family $184,000 to raise a baby from birth to age seventeen.

As you might imagine, the more money you make, the more money you tend to spend raising your kids. So this $184,000 figure jumps dramatically with higher income levels. The cost to raise a child does not decline dramatically at lower income levels either. The USDA reports that families making less than $42,000 spend roughly $135,000 raising each child from birth to age seventeen.

That's *a lot* of money. This is why it's so important to talk about the financial impact of having children. Before, during, and after pregnancy, it's vital to keep referring back to the gross income pie on page 82 to make sure it reflects the changing needs of your family. If your budget is already tight but you want to have another child, it will likely be time to think creatively about what kinds of tradeoffs you can make to achieve your goals. We know of families who (quite literally) have chosen to turn their living rooms into group bedrooms to affordably house their growing flock of kiddies. At the other end of the spectrum, we know couples who have deliberately put off starting a family until they have their financial house in better order. There are no right or wrong answers here. The key is just to make conscious, deliberate choices. Remember, the whole point of Getting Financially Naked is to reduce financial stress. The bottom line is that as your family grows, it becomes increasingly important to stay on top of your finances.

ASK YOURSELF AND EACH OTHER THESE QUESTIONS
- How many children do we want?
- How does our household income match up against our desired family size?
- What tradeoffs can we make to achieve our dream family?

As any parent will tell you, the years fly by quickly. One day you are juggling diapers and bottles, and the next thing you know your children are asking if they can borrow the car to go out. The early years of parenting can be incredibly hectic. There is one subject, however, that you want to start thinking about as early on in your child's life as you can—and that is college. The reason is that the money you start saving early on in your child's life will have the most time to grow.

To Pay or Not to Pay for College?

Another hot button as you raise your children will be planning for their higher education. Some of the priciest private schools these days are sporting price tags in excess of $50,000—a year! Many couples find themselves having philosophical differences here.

Veronica and Vernon are a classic example. They both shared a strong belief in the importance of education, and were thrilled when their daughter Tasha had been accepted at every single college she had applied to. However, they faced a conflict about who should pay for it. While they did not have a college savings fund for Tasha, they did have some taxable savings and sizable 401(k) plans. They went to a financial planner who advised them to save for their retirement first, and to have Tasha take out loans to pay for her education herself. The planner noted kids can get scholarships for school, but parents can't get them for retirement. Fully informed with what the consequences would be, they made the decision to pay for half of Tasha's education—even though it meant pushing off retirement for much longer than they had hoped. Tasha would take on loans for the rest. Veronica and Vernon's story is just one of many. How—or If—you'll finance your children's education is a highly personal decision.

How Much Is Too Much Student Loan Debt?

Lately we've been hearing story after story of students graduating from college with over $150,000 of debt—and entering careers that have incomes that are likely to cap out at $50,000. What that means in plain English is that these young adults will be paying off those student loans for well over thirty years. A rough rule of thumb is this: Be wary of your child taking on more in total debt than what you can expect for his or her average *annual* earnings over their first ten years out of school. For example, if you expect your child to earn an average of $50,000 a year in their first ten years of working, you want to think long and hard about taking on more than $50,000 of debt.

Let's talk next about Joline. She critically thought through the facts to make the decision that was right for her. Joline excelled at pretty much anything she put her mind to. She was accepted into two great colleges—one state and one private. The package offered by the state school would require her to take on around $20,000 of student loans over the course of a four-year degree program. The private school package required loans of closer to $100,000. Initially, Joline wasn't going to consider the financial impact in her choice, thinking that educational debt is "good debt." But when her aunt explained the financial impact, and with Joline knowing her desired career choice would likely end up paying her about $50,000 a year, she decided to go to the public school. Her aunt explained that setting aside 10 percent of her before-tax salary to pay off debt would be reasonable. She suggested that paying that debt off for more than ten years would be a huge burden. Doing the math, Joline realized that it would take her roughly four years to pay off public school versus a whopping twenty years for the private school. For more about saving money for educational needs, we recommend visiting *www.SavingForCollege.com.*

ASK YOURSELF AND EACH OTHER THESE QUESTIONS

- Whom do we feel should pay for college—parents, children, or a combination?
- If we are going to pay for some, or all, of our children's education, what is our savings game plan for those expenses?
- What financial tradeoffs would we need to make to reach our college savings goals?

For years, it was taken as a given that you can't go wrong spending money on higher education. These days, the cost of college and graduate school has grown much faster than wages. This is significant because it means that you really have to think long and hard about how high is too high for the cost of higher education.

Power Step #5: Ask Yourself, "What Financial Obligations Do We Have to All Our Loved Ones?"

The discussion of money and family is not limited to the children you and your honey have together. Remember, your honey didn't just appear on this planet out of thin air. We're talking about parents, siblings, cousins, and even children and ex-spouses from previous marriages. When you consider your extended family—whatever this means to you and your mate—you will realize there's much more opportunity for tension than what first meets the eye.

Let's consider some of the possible scenarios. Has someone in your or your partner's family asked to borrow money from the two of you? Does one of you have elderly parents or siblings in need of financial assistance? Are there children from a previous marriage who have certain expectations? While these situations do not lend themselves to black and white rules, in this last section we'll raise some questions that will help you and your mate traverse what can be a financial and emotional minefield.

WHEN FOR BETTER OR FOR WORSE . . .
REALLY MEANS JUST THAT!

When Jamie met Joe, her heart literally skipped a beat. He was, hands down, the man of her dreams. Joe felt the same and a year later, they were married. We'd like to say it ended there . . . happily ever after. But it didn't. This was Jamie's first marriage and

Joe's second. Joe had four teenage children from a previous marriage and they seemed to think their dad was a bottomless piggy bank. Having grown up in a very frugal family, Jamie was driven nuts by the constant request for material possessions from Joe's kids. Because they did not Get Financially Naked before getting married, this issue came as a shock to both of them. The tensions ran so high that Jamie and Joe ended up having to seek marital therapy to help preserve their marriage. Thankfully, their commitment to their relationship enabled them to work through this rough patch and stay married.

One huge area of tension in marriages is how to treat requests from family members for financial help. The examples run the gamut. In addition to the most common questions surrounding education for your children, here are some of the ones we've heard lately:

- A father (with a bad credit score) wanting his daughter to buy a house in her name and let him pay rent to her to cover the mortgage.
- The adult child of a couple asking to move back home because she didn't like having roommates—which she'd have to have financially if she lived on her own.
- The college freshman who wants mom and dad to buy her a brand new ($50,000!) car.
- The elderly parents who can no longer take care of themselves and need assistance.

When you get in a committed relationship, you are taking on more than just your mate. You are taking on his or her family as well. Money issues are always tricky, but become all the more so when they involve close family members. Here are some questions we suggest asking each other:

ASK YOURSELF AND EACH OTHER THESE QUESTIONS:

- **Children:** If there are children from previous marriages, are there any areas of financial commitments that we should discuss?
- **Parents:** Have we talked to them about their own financial situation? Are they prepared for retirement? Do they have sufficient medical coverage? What help might they need from us and what are we willing and able to afford to do?
- **Siblings and other family members:** What kind of relationship do we have here? What needs might they have? What are we willing (and unwilling) to do to help siblings and other family members?

The approach you take toward requests for financial help within the family will be highly personal. Cultural, religious, and plain old practical considerations make this subject tough to generalize. That said, we think there are two solid approaches you can take to help mitigate tension when it comes to money and family.

Option #1 for Loaning to Family Members

If you decide to loan money, write it off in your head. Your relationships are more important than the money. If you can't afford to lose it, just say no. Otherwise, you risk losing both your money and, more importantly, the relationship.

Option #2 for Loaning to Family Members

If you feel strongly that you want to loan money and get it back, make it formal. Create a legal document. You can get inexpensive do-it-yourself loan kits at *www.Nolo.com.* There are even websites where you can arrange for a third party to handle the logistics such as *www.VirginMoneyUs.com.*

Where Will the Five Power Steps Take You?

Each of the topics discussed in Chapter 5 and Chapter 6 can be—and in fact are—the subjects of entire books. Our goal with these two chapters has been to get you and your mate talking about five key areas in a couple's life that, left unaddressed, can cause stress, tension, and even long-standing grudges to develop. A little discussion about these topics early on can go a long way toward ensuring the financial stability and well-being of your whole family.

PART C

TIME TO GET TACTICAL

CHAPTER SEVEN

Save Wisely for Your Financial Goals

Them here are some who might argue it's no small irony that "save" is a four-letter word. When we ask people to free associate with the word "saving," we get all kinds of answers, most of which relate to deprivation and feeling constrained. Ironically, the practice of routinely saving money is about achieving freedom and spending that money down the road.

Amy and Matt's experience is an example of why saving is so powerful. Amy and Matt love each other dearly, but they both hate their jobs. They each work more than sixty hours a week and have no time or energy to look for new jobs. Because they are working so hard, they feel like they should be able to buy what they want when they want it, but as a result, they currently have nothing in savings. They feel trapped because they are living paycheck-to-paycheck. And Amy and Matt are not alone.

If the entire nation were asked to Get Financially Naked, you'd be stunned at the view. A shocking number of people, across the income spectrum, are lacking even the most basic level of financial protection: a savings cushion. From the 1950s through the early 1980s, we Americans were pretty good savers, socking away an average of 10 percent of our incomes each year. But something happened on the way to the new millennium—complete consumer craziness. Over the past twenty-five years, we witnessed a super-sizing of our consumptive appetites that has left many of us financially obese and bloated with debt. It appears as if the time-honored American tradition of thrift has gone into hibernation. How did this happen? Well, before we talk about that, let's talk about *your* personal attitude toward saving. Answer these questions by writing down whatever pops into your head when you first read it—and ask your mate to do the same. These exercises can be done together or separately on different sheets of paper. And don't forget to wait to share your responses until *both* of you have completed the exercise.

When you hear the word S-A-V-E, what comes to mind?

_____

_____

_____

_____

_____

_____

_____

Now ask your partner to do the same exercise.

_____

_____

_____

_____

_____

_____

How can saving make *your* life better?

_____

_____

_____

_____

_____

_____

_____

_____

If the word "S-A-V-E" conjured up thoughts of deprivation and made you think it was no small irony that it is a four-letter word, you are not alone. Millions of people feel this way at first. If you need a stronger motivator to shift your impression of saving, consider this:

> Contrary to popular belief, saving is actually about spending money—just in the future, not right now.

Knowledge Is Power

The truth is that millions of people feel lost when it comes to saving. You might not know how much you should be trying to save or what that money will be used for in the future. When you don't know what you should be doing and why, you often adopt a default attitude of ignorance is bliss and just hope everything will work out okay.

However, without a clear financial roadmap for saving, all too many people simply live it up, going from one paycheck to the next. After all, if you are in a store and see the latest electronic gizmo, but you don't have a savings plan firmly in your head before you go out shopping, the odds are very high that you will spend more than you should. And if all of your friends and coworkers are doing the same, well, the odds are even higher.

We've seen this behavior time and again. The good news is that once you are making a livable wage, saving is really about a mindset. We know people who can manage to save money routinely on annual incomes of $30,000 a year and people who say they can't find anything left to save on annual incomes of $300,000—*or more*—a year. You can start with any amount, and as your savings start to accumulate, you'll have something to feel very proud about. With that background, let's move on to the nuts and bolts of saving.

The Three Reasons You Save Money

This is a book about Getting Financially Naked, so we're going to ask you some intimate questions about your personal savings situations. First, however, let's talk about each of the three key reasons you save: for an emergency fund, for big-ticket items, and for retirement.

The Power of an Emergency Fund

Simply put, an emergency fund is step one in living your life from a position of financial strength. Having one gives you the power to choose jobs and partners for the right reasons. Emergencies come in all shapes and sizes. Here are a few we've heard of recently. These examples aren't meant to flat out scare you, but rather to make you aware of the possible unexpected situations that arise. Too many of us think, "Oh, nothing will happen to me," but consider these stories and you might think a bit differently:

- $500 for unexpected car repairs
- $750 for medical bills not covered by insurance plan
- $325 for a sky-high utility bill caused by a faulty air conditioner
- $3,000 for roof repairs after a major hurricane
- $1,000 for a pet parakeet's life-saving surgery

If you don't have one already, your goal is to create an emergency fund as soon as possible. Without a basic cushion, you are setting yourself up to experience financial stress when an unexpected expense comes up.

To truly live from a position of financial strength, you'll need to have *at least* three to six months of essential living expenses tucked away in an emergency fund. While this may seem an overwhelming goal at first, the key is to get started. Even a small cushion can go a long way toward helping reduce financial stress. With time and commitment, you can get there. It's no different from deciding you want to run a marathon. You don't start out running the full twenty-six miles, you start off with a single step.

This level of savings will provide you with a solid cushion in case you or your mate lose—or want to quit—your job. Note: If you or your mate work in jobs that have uncertain incomes, or are at risk for layoffs, you'll want to make sure that your savings cushion is enough to cover six to twelve months of essential living expenses.

Saving for Life's Big-Ticket Items

The second reason you save is for what we call "big-ticket" items. These are things like a down payment on a car, a down payment on a house, a wedding, or education for yourself or your children. We'd all love to be able to pull out our checkbook and pay for these kinds of expenses out of pocket, but the reality for most of us is that we have to save up for these big-ticket items.

This area can really trip people up. In the good old days— before the widespread use of credit cards and easy access to credit—people had to save up for these kinds of expenditures. With the financial crisis of 2008–2009, it seems we are getting back to basics where you have to have a sizeable down payment before you can buy a car or a home. We think that's a very good thing indeed.

Drinking—Instead of Serving—a Margarita on the Beach in Your Golden Years

The final reason you save may seem as relevant to your current life as getting your toes shortened to fit into pointy toe stilettos. It's for your retirement. Now if you are like most people, you can see why it makes sense to save for emergencies. You can also probably see why it makes sense to save up for big-ticket items like a down payment on a car or house. But retirement, heck, that's years down the road. You have career ladders to climb, an exciting life to lead today, so why focus on or save for retirement *now*?

The answer is the power of time. Time is like a special fertilizer for your money. The longer you take your saved money and invest it (we'll talk more about investing in the next chapter), the more opportunity you give it to grow and to be there for you when you need it in retirement. To illustrate just how powerful this process can be, let's imagine that on the day you are born you received a "magic" $100 bill. What's magic about this $100 bill is that every ten years it doubles. Look at the chart on the following page to see what you'd have over time.

When you invest your savings wisely, this is what happens to your money. It grows over time. Importantly, not only do you increase the amount you have to spend in the future, but you also dramatically reduce the amount of financial stress in your life right now. And we've yet to meet a single person who enjoys being stressed out about money.

The vast majority of people we talk to want money to be an enabler, a tool that gives them the power to lead the life they want to live. If you had a choice, at what age would you want to receive this magic $100 bill? Why, as early as pos-

BEHOLD THE POWER OF COMPOUNDING

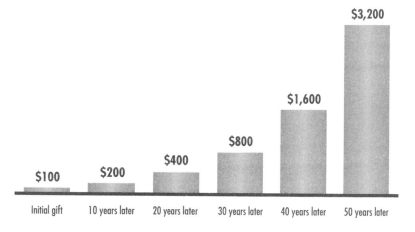

*Example assumes average annual return of 7%

sible, of course, because the more time it has to double, the more money you end up with. This is exactly the reason why you want to start saving for your retirement early. The earlier you start saving and investing, the more you'll end up with in your nest egg. Starting early makes a huge difference. If you haven't started early, all is not lost. The point is to look forward.

Tomorrow's Retirement Is Different from Today's Retirement

Retirement savings today is much more important than it was for our parents and grandparents. Why? We are living much longer in retirement than they did, and we don't have the same sources of traditional retirement income—namely old-style pensions where you received a monthly check from your company for life. Instead, our generation will have to pay for the bulk of our retirement out of our own savings.

Knowing How Much to Save

Now that we've laid out the three reasons you save money, you're probably wondering how much of your hard-earned money to set aside for each of your three savings goals. We've heard countless people tell us that they want to save, but they just don't know where to begin.

KEEP IT SIMPLE
Strive to save 15 percent of your before-tax income.

- Five percent will go toward your emergency fund and big-ticket items combined.
- Ten percent will go toward your retirement savings.

If these numbers cause you some financial heartburn, remember, knowledge is power. This is your goal. Even if you can't possibly get there today—and many people can't—just remember that with time and commitment, you can get there over time. The real key to financial success is having a long-term financial roadmap and the courage to tough it out.

Getting Financially Naked About Your Savings

In Chapter 4 you learned about your—and your mates'—level of knowledge, interest, and behavior when it comes to saving money. In Chapters 5 and 6 you learned about some of the real life situations where those savings would come in handy. Now it's time to take all this to the next level and dig a little deeper. To make this information you've gleaned in previous chapters truly powerful, you've got to *act* on it. That's exactly what we're going to do next.

This next step can quite literally change your life, so we ask you to set some time aside to focus on it. You are about to collect some basic financial information and use it to create the life you really want to live. If you are not seriously committed yet, collect this data for you individually. If you have merged accounts, are living together, or are married, you'll want to do the following based on your combined finances. Doing this exercise on a combined basis will be all the more important if you are doing The Financial Three Way—Yours, Mine, and Ours. You can download extra copies of this worksheet at *www .GetFinanciallyNaked.com.*

How much in *total* savings do you have today? How much of that savings is in your day-to-day bank account? If you have other accounts (e.g., IRA, taxable brokerage account), how much of your savings is stored there?

_____

_____

_____

_____

_____

_____

_____

What are you saving this money for?

_____

_____

_____

_____

_____

How long would your savings last you in an emergency?

_____

_____

_____

_____

_____

How much are you currently saving this year as a percent of your before-tax income?

_____

_____

_____

_____

_____

_____

OKAY, NOW IT'S TIME TO DEBRIEF. HERE ARE SOME QUESTIONS TO DISCUSS WITH YOUR HONEY.

• What did you discover?
• Were you surprised?
• How close are you to your savings goals?

No matter where you are—yes, even if your answer to each of the previous questions was zero—we're going to help you make progress by identifying money drains.

Identifying Your Money Drains

If you are still thinking there's no way you can possibly find money to save—stick with us. We're now going to give you three incredibly powerful tools to help you identify your money drains.

- Eliminating "credit carditis" from your life forever.
- Asking, "How bad do I want it?"
- Knowing your cash flow.

Eliminating Credit Carditis

The first step is to look inside your wallet. No, not to see how much cash you have, but to see how many credit cards you have. But first—yes, you see the pattern here—we'll ask you a few questions:

How many plastic cards do you have (including credit, debit, retail store, and gas cards)? Name each one here:

_____

_____

_____

_____

_____

_____

Do you know the interest rate on each one of your cards? If not, please go look them up and write it down here.

_____

_____

_____

_____

_____

_____

Do you carry a balance? If yes, what is the total amount of that balance across all your cards?

_____

_____

_____

_____

_____

We like to call having too many credit cards *credit carditis.* Most people are, in fact, addicted to credit, having an average of fifteen pieces of plastic in their wallet. The harsh reality is that credit card debt can be as addictive and debilitating as drugs or gambling. Used wisely—which means paying your monthly balance off on time and in full every month—credit cards can be your best friend. Used wisely, they not only provide the convenience of not having to carry around wads of cash, but they can also help you build a good credit history. Used poorly—by having too many cards or carrying a balance from month to month—credit cards can turn on you faster than you think.

If you are like most Americans, you may be reading this thinking, "Great, what do I do now? I'm sitting on a small mountain of credit card debt!" First, do not beat yourself up. Leading your life from a position of financial strength is all about looking forward, not backwards. Remember, no one can go back, so know that you are not alone. It's about making empowering decisions with an eye to your future. The first thing you need to do is set a goal for yourself. Actually, we can set it for you! Your goal is to pay off your credit card debt as fast as possible. Why is this so important?

> If you have a typical credit card with a mid-teens interest rate and a 3 percent minimum monthly payment and you're not paying your bill in full each month, this means you are effectively *doubling* the price of whatever you put on that card.

So those $50 jeans you put on your credit card and paid off over time just ran you 100 big ones. If you have credit card debt right now, your aim is to pay it off as fast as possible, starting with your highest interest rate card.

The good news about paying off your credit cards is that adding some extra money to your payment every month goes a long way toward reducing the interest you will be paying, and gets your debt paid off a lot faster.

HERE ARE SOME BASIC RULES OF THUMB TO USE TO PAY OFF YOUR CREDIT CARD DEBT

- If you have $5,000 or less of credit card debt, pay an extra $50 a month above your minimum required payment.
- If your balance is $5,000 to 10,000, add $100 a month.
- If it's more than $10,000, add $150 a month.

How to Reduce Your Stack of Plastic

Aim to take your household's stack of plastic and reduce it to the two to three cards you are going to keep. Keep the cards with the lowest interest rate and annual fee (in that order). Although it might seem scary to cut down, fewer cards actually allow you to track where your money is going and stick to your budget.

How Bad Do I Want It?

The second potential money drain is not understanding the relationship between the money you spend and how hard you had to work to earn that money. If you are not able to save 15 percent of your income today, we're going to give you a powerful tool to help you get closer to your goal. It's called How Bad Do You Want It? Let's look at Sheila's example to see how it works.

YOU WORK HARD FOR YOUR MONEY

Sheila makes $40,000 a year. She works a standard forty-hour work week, and pays 25 percent in taxes. This translates into roughly $15 an hour after tax that she gets to take home for every hour she works. That means if she wants to buy a pair of jeans for $150, it will take her ten hours of work to be able to pay for it. Armed with this, Sheila can now ask herself, "How bad do I want it?"

Next time you have the urge to splurge, do the math, and then ask yourself, "How bad do I want it?"

WHAT'S YOUR HOURLY AFTER-TAX INCOME?

Annual Income	Annual Taxes	What's Left to Spend After Taxes	Hourly After-Tax Income*
$10,000	$2,500	$7,500	$4
$20,000	$5,000	$15,000	$8
$30,000	$7,500	$22,500	$11
$40,000	$10,000	$30,000	$15
$50,000	$12,500	$37,500	$19
$60,000	$15,000	$45,000	$23
$70,000	$17,500	$52,500	$26
$80,000	$20,000	$60,000	$30
$90,000	$22,500	$67,500	$34
$100,000	$25,000	$75,000	$38

*Assumes a 25 percent effective tax rate and a 2,000 hour work year.

Know Your Flow

If the concept of the gross income pie that we introduced on page 82 was new to you, you are not alone. Most people have no idea how much their lives really cost them. Studies have shown that when forced to estimate, most of us put forth figures that are 10 to 20 percent less than what we really spend.

Given this tendency to habitually underestimate our expenses, another powerful tool is what we call the Financial Reality Check. To do this, simply slip a piece of paper or a small notebook in your wallet, and for two months write down every single thing you spend money on. At the end of each month, take out two different colored highlighters. In one color, highlight all your needs—the things you *have* to have like housing, food, transportation, insurance, and child care—and in another color highlight all your wants—the fun stuff. Now take a close look at each category to see if you can cut back on anything. For instance, you may find that you sleep much better at night by cutting out your fancy gym membership, buying a jump rope, and having the extra money go to your credit card debt. But the only way you'll know for sure is to take a hard look at where your money is flowing. If you need some additional inspiration, read on.

INSPIRATION FROM OTHERS

When Beverly and John first learned that they should be saving at least 10 percent of their income for retirement, they thought, "Get real, that's not going to happen in our lifetime!" Then a friend suggested that they take any raises and devote them to their retirement savings. Within a few years, Beverly and John had not only met, but had actually exceeded their savings goals.

Grace wanted her wedding to be a day she'd always remember—and not because it took an eternity to pay it off. Grace and her fiancée come from large, warm families, so there were 200 people to invite. They sat down together, created a budget, and did all sorts of creative things to stick to it—from having a potluck dinner to sending out electronic wedding invitations. Their wedding was unique, with many guests saying it was the best they'd attended. The even better part, it actually came in under budget. More fun, less money—what a deal!

Margaret is a single mom with three teenage children. A loving parent, it was important to her that her kids not want for anything. But the love was coming at a steep price, as the cost of lessons, clothes, outings, etc., added up. At a friend's urging, Margaret decided to hold a family summit and share with her kids some of the financial pressures she was feeling. She told them how much as a family they had to spend each week on food and fun. She suggested they decide together as a family how to allocate funds going forward in these areas. To her surprise, the kids had already sensed she was tense and jumped into the family project with both feet. The result is that she's back on budget and, more importantly, the shared responsibility has brought her family closer.

Saving's Bottom Line

The bottom line is saving money is all about balancing the desire to live well today with the need to save and invest for the future. So every time you think you're *depriving* yourself of something you want in the moment, think how you are really *awarding* yourself with the opportunity for a more comfortable, safer, and better future. After saving, the next key to financial security and success is investing wisely. We'll cover that in the next chapter.

CHAPTER EIGHT

Invest Your Hard-Earned Money So It Works Hard for You

W e know it's hard to save money. We're not going to try to suggest otherwise. Once you've gone through all that effort to build a cash stash, it's natural to want to make sure you are doing the best you can with it. You've probably heard that it's a good thing to invest and make your money work for you. But what does that really mean? The answer to this seemingly simple question has caused more than a few fights between couples. There typically are three underlying reasons for these arguments.

The first is that different people have different goals for their savings and different appetites for risk—a.k.a. the "how-well-can-you-sleep-at-night" test—for their investments. For instance, one thirty year old may want to invest aggressively with hopes of retiring at fifty-five, while another thirty year old may prefer a slow-and-steady course, happy to work well into his or her seventies if need be. One person in a couple might feel a deep urge to really go for it and try to find that one investment in a million that will pay off big time, while the other may want to tuck all that hard-saved money under a mattress. Our point is that just because Cupid strikes, it does not mean you will have similar approaches to investing.

Second, in observing countless couples, we've noticed that the person with more interest in investing tends to take ownership of that financial task. Sometimes the partner with the greater degree of interest in investing doesn't fully communicate with the other partner about what's going on with their joint funds. That in turn can lead to big problems because, not only is there a lack of communication, but:

An interest in investing does not always lead to success at investing.

Last, but perhaps most important of all, investing is a subject that intimidates many people. As women who have worked for more than twenty combined years in the financial services industry, we can tell you from firsthand experience that most people think you need a super sophisticated investment strategy to be successful. Ironically, the real secret to investing more often than not is to just *keep it simple.*

When we talk about investing as being a potential major source of tension in relationships, we are not talking theoretically. Take the case of Kit. Kit is a very successful lawyer who let her husband manage the family finances because he didn't have a job and it made him feel busy and important to manage their investments. Long story short, Kit's husband ended up day trading away all of their retirement savings. They are now divorced. Today Kit is in her sixties, starting over both emotionally and financially. Kit allowed us to share her story because she wants you to learn from her experience so this doesn't happen to you.

As with virtually every aspect of a relationship, once again the key to success is communication. If either one of you is uncertain about or uncomfortable with how your money is being invested, hearing, "It's okay, just trust me," from your partner is not going to cut it.

YOUR INVESTMENTS MAY BE IN JEOPARDY IF:
- Your partner responds to questions by saying, "Just trust me," with no further explanation.
- Your partner's favorite source of investment tips is from the guys/the gals on the golf course.

- Your investment portfolio has more than 100 individual stocks (and neither you or your partner are investment professionals).
- Your portfolio activities include sophisticated strategies such as *short selling* and buying *naked options* (but you and your partner have no formal training in investing).*

Note: These are just examples. Sadly, there are plenty of other reasons your investments could be in jeopardy.

It's time to start Getting Financially Naked when it comes to your personal investments. Let's begin with a quick assessment of your current investments.

Do you know where your money is invested? If so, list the various institutions where you have accounts.

_____

_____

_____

_____

_____

_____

_____

_____

_____

_____

_____

_____

Do you know *how* your money is invested? (By this, we mean do you know what specific stocks, bonds, or mutual funds you own.) If so, summarize your situation below.

_____

_____

_____

_____

_____

_____

_____

_____

_____

_____

Do you know the current value of your investments? If so, list each account and its current total value here.

_____

_____

_____

_____

_____

_____

_____

_____

_____

_____

_____

Your answers to the preceding three questions give you a fantastic jumping off point to talk about investing with your honey.

> If you do not know where your money is, how it is invested, or what it is currently worth, now's as good a time as any to get down and dirty with your investments.

In order to have an informed conversation with your mate about your investments, it's important to have a basic understanding of investing. These next pages will give you the nuts and bolts of what you need to know to start a productive conversation with your honey about investing. Let's begin with our quick crash course in "Investing 101."

Investing 101: Why Go There?

First, let's talk about why on earth you would want to invest in the first place. Given the dramatic swoon of the global stock markets from their 2007 highs, followed by the multiple bank and financial institution failures of 2008, it's an increasingly common thought to want to just stash those hard-earned dollars in a nice, solid steel safe (we're not kidding, while sales of many consumer goods have gone down, sales of safes have gone up). Ironically, money tucked away in that state-of-the-art safe may be inaccessible to human thieves but unsafe nonetheless. How's that? Well, here's a question for you:

What do you think would happen to the value of your money if you put $100 in your safe for thirty years? When you opened that door three decades later you'd still have $100. But when you went out to spend that $100 you'd find out that it would only buy what $40 buys today. To add insult to injury, this example assumes inflation—the harsh reality that prices tend to go up over time—runs in line with the historical average of roughly 3 percent. There's always the possibility that inflation

THE BIG BITE OF INFLATION

What $100 is worth in 30 years at various rates of inflation

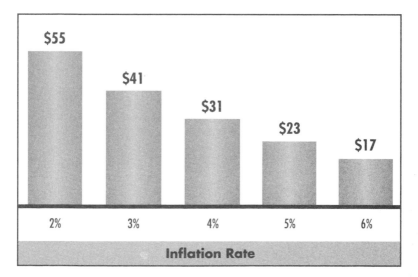

$55	$41	$31	$23	$17
2%	3%	4%	5%	6%

Inflation Rate

going forward could be significantly higher. The graphic on the previous page shows just how big the bite inflation takes out of your spending power can be in response to seemingly small increases in the rate of inflation.

As scary as the uncertainties of investing may be, the probability that inflation will erode the purchasing power of your money over time if you do nothing with it is very high indeed.

As with your health, there are no guarantees. But your odds of being healthier are markedly higher by eating right and exercising. The same goes for investing. That's why you want to go there.

Investing 101: Where Do We Start?

A top-notch investment plan begins with you and your mate asking three surprisingly straightforward questions. Don't over think these, just answer them honestly!

- When do we need to spend our money?
- What is each of our gender and current age?
- What is our appetite for risk (that make-sure-you-can-sleep-at-night factor)?

Your answers to these three questions, combined with the three keep-it-simple rules we present next, will enable you to create the investment mix that is right for you. As with all investment advice, it's important to tailor it to your specific situation.

Keep-It-Simple Rule #1

If you have known expenses in the next five years, protect that money against inflation using *cash equivalents.*

Any money that you know you must spend over the next five years should not be considered money you are investing. Investing by its very nature involves tradeoffs. The whole point of investing is that in exchange for taking on some risk you get the potential, but not the guarantee, of an attractive return. Thus, by its very nature, an investment is not safe. If you know you have to spend money in the next few years, you don't want to subject it to investment risk. Rather, your goal should be to protect it against the ravages of inflation. The most straightforward way to do this is to put that money in cash equivalents. These are savings accounts, money market funds, or certificates of deposit. (Note: Make sure the institution you select is FDIC or SIPC insured—if in doubt, just ask them.)

Brittany Meets an Unsafe Investment

Brittany invested $50,000 in a safe, blue chip company in 2007 with money that she planned to use for graduate school in 2010. Alas, by 2009 that 100-year-old company had seen its stock price decline over 50 percent, and Brittany's safe investment of $50,000 had shrunk to a mere $25,000. (Brittany assumed this company's stock would be safe because the company had been in business for so many years.)

If you have five or more years on your side, now you are ready to invest that hard-earned money so it works for you. This brings us to our next rule of thumb.

Keep-It-Simple Rule #2

For money you will not need to spend for at least five years, the maximum percentage of money you should have in stocks is 110 minus your age if you are female, and 100 minus your age if you are male.

At the simplest level, you have three choices for investing your longer-term money: real estate, bonds, and stocks. Over the very long run—and by that we mean over the last eighty to 100 years—stocks have generated the highest return, followed by bonds, followed by real estate. Here's a bit more information about the long-run returns of the past:

- Stocks have generated a total return of roughly 10 percent per year *on average* for the past eighty plus years. (But put on your seatbelt because it's a bumpy ride—historically the market has gone down in more than one out of every four years.)
- Bonds have generated a total return of just north of 5 percent per year *on average*.
- Real estate—after you factor in all the associated costs—has appreciated just over 3 percent per year *on average*. We highlight the issue of the associated real estate expenses (property tax, insurance, utilities, upkeep—all things your stock and

bond investments don't have), because in the 2003 to 2007 period, all too many Americans were lulled into the belief that real estate was the ultimate safe investment.

HOME, SOUR, HOME . . .
Grace and George are two very smart people with successful careers. They felt confident in their future earnings potential, so to make a little extra money they bought a rental property. Their thinking was that the income generated by their tenants' monthly rent payments would result in a nice, steady contribution to their nest egg. Unfortunately, their tenants didn't pay on time and caused all sorts of damage to the rental property, resulting in significant, unexpected out-of-pocket costs for Grace and George.

So how do you decide what mix of stocks, bonds, and real estate is right for your portfolio? A powerful, yet keep-it-simple approach takes into consideration your gender and your age.

Over the past eighty-plus years, stocks have had the highest long-run investment return. While there is no guarantee that history will repeat itself, we still like stocks for the long run. However, when you invest in the stock market, you need to know that you are potentially in for a very bumpy ride. As we referenced earlier, since 1926 the stock market has lost money in over one out of every four years. That's why the more time you have on your side, the better when it comes to investing in stocks. The gender and age-based rule of thumb—Keep-It-

Simple Rule #2—is designed to keep a person with an average risk tolerance from having too much of their hard-earned savings in stocks.

For instance, Nancy is a thirty-year-old woman. Using the keep-it-simple rule of thumb, the maximum Nancy should own in stocks is 80 percent (110 - 30 = 80). In case you are wondering, the reason for the difference in calculations for women versus men is that statistically speaking, women live an average of seven years longer than men, and thus need a little extra juice to make sure they don't outlive their savings.

As with all financial advice, your ultimate decision about the mix of stocks, bonds, real estate, and cash in your portfolio will be highly personal. These rules of thumb are not intended to be black and white, ironclad directives, but rather guideposts to judge whether or not you are heading off the reservation. When it comes to talking money with your honey, it is essential to make the decisions that work for your particular circumstances. This brings us to our final rule of thumb.

Keep-It-Simple Rule #3

Your personal risk tolerance will determine how well you sleep at night. Let's say you have a very low risk tolerance. If it's going to make you physically ill as a thirty-year-old woman to put 80 percent of your long-term money in stocks, then don't do it. That said, you'll also want to bear in mind that there will be consequences. You may sleep better now, but down the road, the sheets may get a bit threadbare because your investments weren't aggressive enough to offset inflation and maintain your purchasing power. If, by contrast, you have a high-risk tolerance and want to dial up your exposure to stocks, you'll want to remember that if you are wrong, you can end up on those same threadbare sheets. This is our way of saying that the right mix in your portfolio between stocks, bonds, real estate (which for most people, their main home represents more than enough exposure to), and cash—depends on both squishy and hard factors (i.e., both your emotions/beliefs and some basic math).

Investing 101: How Do We Do It?

Investing, on the surface, can seem like a very complex process. For years, Carmen put off dealing with investing because she thought to be successful she'd have to go out and buy stock in the next Google or Microsoft, or identify exactly what kind of bonds to put in her portfolio. That's a pretty intimidating expectation. It's no wonder that Carmen felt frozen with uncertainty and defaulted to a do nothing position, keeping her money in cash.

Unless you want to analyze companies for a living, the best way to invest in stocks and bonds is by buying a whole basket of them—or a mutual fund—as opposed to trying to cherry-pick a specific handful.

In the world of investing, these baskets are called mutual funds. We like mutual funds that don't have a lot of buying and selling going on and charge you a very low fee. These are called *index* funds, and while the name may or may not be recognizable to you, the key is to know that they are easy to buy and can be a keep-it-simple and powerful action plan that will likely put you ahead of the vast majority of investors. This includes even the so-called super sophisticated ones.

Another option for investing your retirement savings is a Target Date Retirement Fund. With these funds, you choose a fund for the approximate year when you will retire; it's kind of like a "set it and forget it" rotisserie chicken. These funds shift the mix of what they own over time to take your age into account.

We talked earlier about how you only want to invest money that you don't have to spend for at least five years. For most people, that means they are talking about investing money for their retirement. Typically, that retirement savings is done either through a plan offered at work (common types of such plans include 401(k), 403(b), 457, and thrift savings plans) or individually through an IRA, which stands for Individual Retirement Account. While the names of these accounts can sound cold and scary, the two biggest decisions you have to make are very straightforward: (1) how much money you are going to save each year in them, and (2) how you are going to spread your money between stocks, bonds, and cash—which is a decision that the keep-it-simple rules of thumb from this chapter are designed to help you make.

WATCH OUT FOR THESE CLASSIC RETIREMENT MISTAKES

The three biggest mistakes we see people making with their retirement savings are:

- **Not doing it:** Since you've chosen to Get Financially Naked, this hopefully won't happen to you and your honey.
- **Forgetting to "order off the menu":** By this, we mean you sign up for an employer-sponsored retirement plan such as a 401(k) or 403(b), or you open up an IRA account, but neglect to choose the right investment options for your situation. Signing up for the account is like picking a restaurant to go to for dinner. To have a positive dining experience you'll also need to order wisely off the menu—in this case, it's just a menu of investment options.
- **Forgetting to name or update beneficiaries:** When many people go through life-changing events, like getting married, divorced, or having kids, they neglect to update their beneficiaries for their retirement plans (and life insurance). These updates are vital because, to many people's surprise, the beneficiaries you name on those specific accounts will trump your instructions in your will.

To some of you, these mistakes may be obvious, while to others, maybe you didn't realize you were making them. Let us say, though, that we meet people who make these mistakes every day. For example, we recently met an otherwise savvy person who had all of her retirement money in cash since the early 1990s. Her reasoning was just, well, because *it all seemed a bit much to deal with*. We hear this type of story all the time. Hopefully, these three simple rules of thumb will give you a framework to start talking to your honey about whether you both are comfortable with how your money is currently invested.

A Good Investment of Time

Our goal with this chapter was to get you started talking about this vital subject with your mate. The topic of investing is vast. Entire books have been written on the subject. But we hope you can find a launching pad here. If you'd like to learn more about investing, we suggest reading our previous book, *On My Own Two Feet*.

CHAPTER NINE

Sustain Your Financial Plan

U p until this point, you've done what it takes to Get Financially Naked and work toward financial harmony in your life. Good for you! You have one more critical step on this journey. In order for you to truly live the life that makes your heart sing, you need to find a way to *sustain* your financial plan. We all know how life works—you are busy heading diligently in direction A when life suddenly pulls you into direction B.

Sometimes the twists are great fun. For instance, you may get an unexpected raise and want to make sure it's handled well financially. Other times, they are not so much fun. For example, one of you may be laid off unexpectedly and you need to adjust your spending to reflect the new reality. In short, the one thing you can always expect in life is the unexpected.

> To make sure that your relationship stays on financial track through life's inevitable twists and turns, you must keep your financial dialogue going.

The good news is that we are not talking about doing this daily at the dinner table. However, committing to having a joint check-in at least once a year to review and reassess puts you in a solid position to make the most of life's opportunities and challenges. As for when to do this, it's up to you—you can do it every January, every April after tax day, or on some date that just makes you happy. The only exception is if something truly massive happens (new child, new job, etc.), then you'll want to schedule an extra intra-year check-in.

How does the check-in work? You may be pleasantly surprised at how easy it is. There are three straightforward steps. The whole process should take less than one hour. It starts by going back to the beginning of this book, to the visualization exercise from Chapter 1. We've found that people's answers to this exercise sometimes evolve as their lives evolve Remember there's absolutely no judgment with this exercise—it's neither good nor bad if you stay the same or if you change. It simply is.

Step #1: Get Re-Centered

For step #1 of your annual financial check-in, we'd like to ask you to repeat the visualization from Chapter 1.

When I live my life from a position of financial strength, I will . . .

_____

_____

_____

_____

_____

_____

_____

_____

_____

_____

_____

How does your response compare to what you wrote the last time you did this exercise? Were there any changes? If so, note them here.

_____

_____

_____

_____

_____

_____

_____

_____

_____

_____

Asking these questions each year is vital because over time your priorities and interests may shift. Having an accurate pulse on what is really important to you today keeps your vision and motivation fresh.

Step #2: Reflect & Assess

Step #2 of the periodic check-in process is to pause and think about your financial situation holistically over the past year. We ask you to compare where you were at your last check-in to where you are right now.

OVER THE PAST YEAR . . .

Is there anything you wish you or your partner had done differently, financially speaking? For example, did one of you make a decision that ended up causing financial strife?

_____

_____

_____

_____

_____

_____

_____

_____

Have there been any major changes in the composition of your household (new children, extended family members coming to live with you, etc.)? If so, what changes to your finances have resulted?

_____

_____

_____

_____

_____

_____

_____

_____

_____

What do you think was the best financial move your household made? What kind of discussions and research led you to make that choice, and how can you repeat that going forward?

_____

_____

_____

_____

_____

_____

_____

_____

_____

_____

_____

Is there anything you plan to do differently going forward?

_____

_____

_____

_____

_____

_____

_____

_____

_____

_____

_____

THINKING ABOUT YOUR FINANCES TODAY . . .

Is there any part of your finances that you or your honey are feeling stressed about?

_____

_____

_____

_____

_____

_____

Is there any part of your finances that you would like to learn more about?

_____

_____

_____

_____

_____

Are there any new life goals that you or your honey would like to pursue, and if so, what do you need to do financially to support those goals?

_____

_____

_____

_____

_____

_____

Step #3: Time for the Numbers . . . and a Few Last Questions

We suggest that every year you go back and once again fill out your Get Financially Naked Statement from Chapter 4. (Note: For additional copies of the financial statement, go to *www .GetFinanciallyNaked.com*.) After you've compiled your data, the last piece of the process is to sit down together and discuss the following questions:

- Are any of your or your partner's current financial beliefs at odds with your overarching life goals? If so, what steps can you take to free yourself?
- What changes do you need to make to get there?
- Are you saving what you want? Why or why not? Can revisiting the gross income pie on page 82 help make some often-tough tradeoffs? Can revisiting the Five Power Steps to Financial Success in Chapters 5 and 6 help you find some extra money to save?
- Are your investments doing what you expected? Are there any changes you need to make here?
- Is there anything else specific to your situation that you two would like to work on? For example, paying down debt faster, improving a credit score, making sure you both know where all your important papers are stored, shopping around to see if you can get better rates on your insurance, etc.

We started this book off by sharing some of our own personal money histories, so it only feels right that we end the same way. Here's how the process of Getting Financially Naked has helped us with our honeys—as well as a few words from them so you can really get the full picture.

Manisha's Get Financially Naked Success Story

I married relatively late in life, at age thirty-six, and my husband is older than I am. Coming into our marriage, both my husband and I already had established, successful careers. As such, we were each very much in charge of our own finances. We came to our marriage with many similarities. We're quintessential homebodies. Our idea of a great night together is a pepperoni pizza, a nice bottle of red wine, and a movie. We both love jazz, art films, lollygagging over the Sunday newspaper, and (trying to!) eat healthy and exercise regularly together.

But we did have one area of conflict: money. I thought it was a big conflict. My husband thought it was a small conflict. I am the quintessential squirrel, always worried about the rainy day. My dream is to have enough money that I can live comfortably on the yearly payouts from my investments (interest and dividends). My husband lives more in the moment. He is a big believer that life is not a dress rehearsal. Our age difference may have something to do with the different financial priorities we brought into our marriage. We also have dramatically different levels of interest surrounding money. I (surprise, surprise) find the subject endlessly fascinating. Give me a good personal finance book to curl up with, and I'm in seventh heaven. My husband prefers riding a motorcycle or playing golf, compared to my passion for articles with titles like "Ten ways to lower your utility bills."

Early on in our marriage we would fight (he says "disagree") but only ever about one thing: money. After Getting Financially Naked, however, I now understand where my husband is coming from and he understands me. We've found a system that works perfectly for us. We do The Financial Three Way (mine, yours, ours) with regards to our bank accounts and investments. Because we both came to our marriage with hard-earned assets, we chose to have a prenup (at my request!)—but, most importantly, I have learned that the key to marital harmony on the financial front is compromise. Oh, and not to give my husband the silent treatment when he shares an honest feeling that I didn't want to hear. He has learned that talking freely with me about money, even when he thinks I won't like the news, brings me peace. Now we talk about everything financially without fear or judgment. But it took some work by both of us to get there.

My husband and I spent more on housing, for instance, than I would have spent as a single person. But we are home-bodies. Our home is where we enjoy spending most of our time and do most of our entertaining—and I can now see his point that it's a sound use of our hard-earned savings. He's encouraged me to live a little and allow myself the pleasure of having a beautiful home. In return, I've helped him awaken to the tradeoffs inherent in pursuing a risky investment strategy (you can imagine that a motorcycle rider would have a much higher risk tolerance than a financial squirrel). Consequently, he's made some changes to his investment mix that he now feels really good about. Surprisingly, the best part of all, for both of us, has been the degree to which working through our differences, and finding areas of compromise and similarities financially, has brought us even closer. I feel like we are genuine partners in every sense of the word—and that has to be one of life's greatest gifts.

MANISHA'S HUSBAND, RANDY, SAYS . . .
"At first it was hard. Money was an uncomfortable subject for me, and I preferred to 'run' or remain silent rather talk about it. Manisha likes to see everything in black and white and to know exactly how all the numbers will work. I felt like 'things will take care of themselves' and I didn't understand exactly how the numbers would work—I just knew they would! Once I learned how important discussing our finances was to her, however, I took a deep breath and dove in to the discussion—only to have her react judgmentally at first. Whoops! That really hurt my feelings. One step

forward, two steps back. However, she quickly learned how important it was to me not to have her 'judge' or react angrily to what I had to say, so we both learned something! I now take great pleasure in seeing her eyes light up when I eagerly try to answer any question she asks. It is fun, and has really strengthened our marriage."

Sharon's Get Financially Naked Success Story

When my husband and I got engaged, we merged our finances. We generally saw eye-to-eye when it came to our spending, but he'd occasionally make comments about my purchases. He'd ask me things like, "Why do you need another pair of black pants?" That drove me crazy. At the time, I was in my mid-twenties, working really hard, and doing so because it was important to me to earn my own money and have independence. I resented having any of my purchases questioned, let alone the number of black pants in my closet. Having grown up without the "cool" clothes, this really hit a hot button for me. In fairness to my husband, he was simply trying to make sure our finances were in order (I realized that in retrospect, of course). After a few fights about black pants (!), we realized there was a deeper issue of having mutual trust for each other's decisions when it came to spending what would now be our joint money. We agreed to set a dollar amount below which we would not question each other. It was $250, but we did still tell each other when we had any type of significant expense. For instance, I'd come home and say *yes*, I bought another pair of black pants. Quite honestly, before we really Got Financially Naked and talked about the set dollar amount, I was tempted to hide my shopping bags in the closet. But once things were out in the open, I proudly strutted home with my shopping bags, yes, filled with another pair of black pants or two. That was twelve years ago.

Now that we have two kids, it's all the more important that we are open and honest with each other when it comes to money. Kids are such a huge expense that I can't imagine how we'd handle it without having set up a basic financial system in our home that is based on mutual trust. Without that, we'd probably be fighting a lot more about money. Thank goodness we are not.

SHARON'S HUSBAND, GREG, SAYS . . .

"When we got engaged, it was a big step to merge our finances. It was very helpful to have our open and honest talk about how we approached money. After all, I'm a guy, and a practical one at that. For reference, when we met, I was still wearing the same pants, belts, shirts, and socks that I had from ten years prior. I was probably not the most stylish, but certainly financially prudent. Given that, it was hard for me to understand why my wife-to-be would need yet another pair of pants. Agreeing to a dollar amount below which we could each do what we wanted was liberating for both of us. We both had flexibility and neither one of us wanted to nag each other about money. Once we set up our system, it allowed us to be open with each other regarding our spending."

Getting Financially Naked is rarely easy. For virtually everyone, this money stuff can be hard. We hope with this book, however, we've convinced you that one of the single best investments you can make in yourself and in your relationship is to address this subject head on.

Commonly Asked Questions

The goal of this book is to help you create a solid financial foundation so that you and your honey can talk constructively about your money. We've done a variety of exercises to get you to this point: engaging in some financial foreplay, assessing your financial compatibility, and Getting Financially Naked. We then walked you through the Five Power Steps to Financial Success to ensure your relationship doesn't get torpedoed by financial stress. But you may still have some questions. That's why this section is dedicated to answering some of the most common ones. We've grouped the questions into three broad buckets: Saving, Investing, and Protecting (both yourself and your relationship). So let's jump right in. . . .

Questions about Saving

Q I FEEL I AM CAREFUL WITH MONEY BUT MY MATE LOVES TO GET ON MY CASE ABOUT HOW MUCH I SPEND AT THE GROCERY STORE OR ON GETTING MY HAIR COLORED. IT MAY JUST BE TEASING, BUT IT FEELS LIKE I HAVE TO REPORT IN ON EVERYTHING LIKE A SMALL CHILD. WHAT CAN I DO?

When it comes to spending money, it's important that each person in a relationship feels they have some money that they are allowed to spend with no questions asked. It is just raw human nature to want to have some degree of freedom and control over one's life. If you have joint accounts, the easiest way to do this is to set a dollar amount that each of you is free to spend (or save) each month, no questions asked. That dollar amount will be highly personal. Similarly, you can set a dollar amount above which you both agree to consult each other before spending. More often than not, fights about money occur because one partner felt excluded from the decision. This system helps clarify things up front. You may well have to compromise, but at least you'll have a system in place to resolve disputes.

Q WE'RE MOVING IN TOGETHER AND ARE SERIOUSLY COM-
MITTED TO OUR FUTURE AS A COUPLE. SHOULD WE COM-
BINE BANK ACCOUNTS?

The answer to this question will vary from couple to couple. At present, the vast majority of married couples choose to have joint bank accounts and pay for household expenses out of those joint accounts. However, we've also know of many seriously committed couples doing what we like to call The Financial Three Way. This is our way of saying that a couple chooses to have three buckets of money: mine, yours, and ours. With so many people marrying later in life—after they have accumulated various assets, debt, business, and family obligations—it is becoming more common for a couple to keep their existing separate accounts and then create a new account for joint expenses. A related approach is to share responsibility for joint expenses by simply paying them from each of your individual accounts. The key to success in sharing expenses is once again open communication and a clearly agreed upon game plan that you both feel good about.

If one person makes significantly more than the other does, you may choose to pay for expenses in proportion to how much you contribute to the total household income. For example, if one person makes $60,000 a year and the other makes $40,000 a year, the higher earner would pay 60 percent of joint expenses and the lower earner would pay 40 percent. It is important to note that it's not okay for judgment to be placed by the higher earner on the lower earner. This is all the more important in situations where one spouse is working inside the home—a job that is truly one of the hardest ones there is anywhere. In a loving relationship, you both have equal rights and need to identify jointly what system works best for you both.

Q WE'VE MERGED BANK ACCOUNTS, BUT ARE FIGHTING ABOUT MONEY BECAUSE I'M A SAVER AND MY PARTNER IS A SPENDER. MY PARTNER SAYS, "LIFE'S SHORT AND YOU CAN'T TAKE IT WITH YOU!" WHAT DO I DO?

If someone tells you that you can't have any more chocolate or potato chips—what's the first thing your stomach does? It craves more chocolate or potato chips. Telling your partner not to do something—whether that's spend more or spend less—is not likely to be a very effective move. We've found it to be much more helpful to let your partner know how their spending habits are making you feel about your joint financial life. For instance, you could say—in your own words—something along the lines of, "I love you with all my heart. But when I see the new flat panel TV, MP3 players, and our frequent expensive dinners out, I get scared. I worry that we may not be able to live the life we want in the future because of how we are living today." Now you've turned the situation from an accusation—"You spend like a broken faucet"—to a statement of fact—"The sky is blue." This sets up a more productive conversation.

Alternatively, if you found out while reading Chapter 7 that you two are not meeting your savings goals, this would be another ideal way to raise the subject that spending needs to be reined in. The good news is that having worked through the exercises in Chapter 7, you will likely make a difficult conversation easier. It is also important for you to keep in mind the financial history and financial beliefs that your mate brings to his or her spending habits. Excessive spending may be a sign of another need that is not being met. Clarifying what is *really* driving the excess spending will enable you both to get to the root issue and find a reasonable compromise.

Questions about Investing

Q WE STARTED TO GET FINANCIALLY NAKED BUT MY PARTNER HAS SHUT DOWN, ESPECIALLY AROUND THE SUBJECT OF INVESTING, AND IS REALLY NOT WILLING TO CONTINUE THIS CONVERSATION. WHAT DO I DO?

Typically, when people shut down it is because they are afraid or embarrassed. If you have tried but just can't get through to your honey, you may need outside help from a competent financial adviser. By seeing a financial planner together, you put yourself in a position to ask a neutral third party questions that can help stimulate a more intimate discussion with your mate. For instance, by asking your adviser, "For a couple with our income level, how much should we be saving and how should we be invested?" you open the door to a neutral party making sure you two talk about the key financial questions.

Q HOW CAN I TELL IF A FINANCIAL ADVISER IS ANY GOOD?

A great way to assess a potential financial adviser is to ask your adviser to explain how she or he gets compensated. If your potential adviser dodges the question, that's an immediate red flag. By contrast, reasonable answers include, "I charge you an hourly fee," or "I charge you a percent of your assets under management." What you don't want to hear is someone stammering, turning red, or saying my services don't cost you a thing—because that usually means the cost of those services are embedded in a commission. The one exception to this would be at the large brokerage or mutual fund houses where there is an in-house, salaried staff to advise clients. Next up is knowledge. This can be gleaned through academic degrees and programs. Some of the most respected ones include the CFP (certified financial planner), CPA (chartered public accountant), CPA/PFS (chartered public accountant and personal financial specialist), and CFA (chartered financial analyst). Last but not least, you want to ask your potential adviser about their philosophy with regards to working with clients. Optimal answers include an initial meeting to really understand your current financial picture (what you own, owe, earn, spend, etc.) and your financial goals. You also want to ask them about their philosophy on investing. We personally are partial to financial advisers who focus on low cost, diversified solutions such as index funds, target date retirement funds, and ETFs (exchange traded funds, which are another variant on the old-fashioned index fund).

Q MY MATE THINKS SHE/HE IS THE SECOND INCARNATION OF WARREN BUFFETT. SHE/HE HAS NEVER MET A STOCK TIP THEY DIDN'T LIKE. IT SCARES THE #$%# OUT OF ME, BUT I CAN ALSO SEE THAT MY HONEY IS GETTING GREAT PLEASURE FROM DOING ALL THIS TRADING. WHAT DO I DO?

First, you can remind your honey that Warren is a buy and hold investor of high quality companies. If that doesn't work—and likely it won't if your mate has been bit by the day trading bug—we suggest you agree to a *very small* amount of money that you set aside and quite literally think about as "gambling money." This should be money you can afford to lose. Mentally write it off and let your honey have at it—with the stipulation that under no circumstances is your honey to "short" or "go on margin" (two techniques that could cause you to have to add money to that gambling fund if things turn sour).

Questions about Protecting (Yourself and Your Relationship)

Q I'VE JUST MET THE MOST WONDERFUL PERSON, BUT MY FINANCIAL PAST IS VERY UGLY. WHEN DO I GET FINAN-CIALLY NAKED, AND HOW EXACTLY DO I TELL THIS INCREDIBLE PERSON ABOUT MY FINANCIAL HISTORY?

While there is no magic time frame for Getting Financially Naked, there is a magic ingredient: trust. When you feel you have established a level of trust with each other, then you are ready. If your McDreamy is not willing to get to know all parts of you—the good and the not so good—it's better for you to know that now. You want to be with someone who loves you for who you are and does not make you feel ashamed of actions you have taken in the past that you are working to improve upon now. That said, when you reveal yourself, financially speaking, there is always the possibility that your honey will hear something that just doesn't work for them. While painful, it's better for you both to know this sooner rather than later. As we've said before, financial incompatibility is a relationship killer. As for how to bring it up, there's nothing better than the old-fashioned, "Honey, there's something I'd like to share with you. It's an awkward topic for me to bring up—and it may be a hard one for you to hear. But in the spirit of being open and honest with each other, I'd like to tell you something about my past. Is now a good time for us to have this conversation?"

Q I AM IN THE EARLY PHASES OF DATING SOMEONE. OUR RELATIONSHIP IS NOT SERIOUS ENOUGH TO GET FINAN-CIALLY NAKED YET. SO WHAT ARE THE FINANCIAL RULES? WHO PAYS FOR WHAT?

We often get this question—and not just when people are dating. Believe it or not, we also get it from people who are engaged or even married. By and large, the answer to this question is a highly personal one. For instance, when it comes to dating, some people prefer an old-school style of courtship whereby one partner pays for all outings. By contrast, there are some people who are absolutely insulted by anything less than a 50/50 split of expenses from the get-go in a relationship. The right answer is what feels right in your heart. What's not okay is if you feel your partner isn't pulling their weight or is trying to control you. In an open, loving, and trusting relationship, you should both feel free to bring up the (loaded) topic of money and plan together a system that makes the most sense for both of you. If your partner is unwilling to have this type of conversation, that's a big red flag. As painful as it is (and it is!), better to learn this sooner rather than later.

Q MY PARTNER WAS JUST LAID OFF. IT'S BEEN GUT WRENCH-
ING TO SAY THE LEAST, AND I FEEL BAD BRINGING UP THE
SUBJECT OF MONEY, BUT I'M NERVOUS. WHAT SHOULD I DO?

The loss of a job is one of the most stressful things a person can go through. You are right to want to be as supportive as possible toward your spouse. That said, to fully protect your spouse and your family, it is critical for you to discuss how to adjust your family finances as soon as possible. One of the biggest financial mistakes we see in this situation is families continuing to spend as if they had had no reduction in income. What you choose to cut will be highly personal. The key, however, is that something must give. Go back to the gross income pie in Chapter 5, and assess what areas are most reasonable to adjust for your situation. The process of cutting back can be emotionally painful. It often helps to keep something in the budget that each person truly enjoys to help with the situation. Sometimes a bowl of ice cream or a glass of wine can help too.

These are just a small sampling of the many issues that come up around the subject of Getting Financially Naked. One thing that we've learned while talking about this subject across the country is the power of community. Together we can help each other create a world where money is discussed with the same level of openness that one might discuss what to eat for dinner or what movie to go see. When it comes to Getting Financially Naked, any question is a good question.

Together we can support each other on the path to living each of our lives from a place of financial strength.

Q MY BOYFRIEND/GIRLFRIEND AND I WANT TO BUY A HOUSE. BUT IT'S GETTING TRICKY BECAUSE ONE OF US HAS GREAT CREDIT WHILE THE OTHER ONE'S CREDIT REALLY STINKS. SHOULD WE TRY TO GET A MORTGAGE TOGETHER BASED ON BOTH OF OUR CREDIT SCORES OR JUST IN THE NAME OF THE PERSON WITH THE BEST CREDIT?

First off, let us say that buying property together is serious business. Unless you are in a long-term committed relationship, we think you are opening up a can of worms to buy a home together while "just dating." If the relationship ends, things can (and often do) get really ugly.

There are several key financial issues that arise from your question. The most important is: Why do you want to buy a home together while you are "just dating"? Many people think they "should" buy a home to take advantage of tax benefits or because they've heard it's a "great investment and where real wealth has been made." While these statements can sometimes be true, what is always true is that home ownership comes with a lot of responsibilities and expenses. For instance your annual upkeep costs (insurance, property tax, maintenance, etc.) will typically run around 3% of your purchase price of your home, every year. When you factor in these costs, the "own versus rent" question is not such a lay up. Have you taken this into consideration?

Additionally, if one of you has bad credit—it's important to ask if the behaviors that led to that bad credit have been changed. If they have not, you two are likely not ready for homeownership yet and would be better off not buying until both of your finances are in solid shape. That all said, if you are absolutely dead set on buying a home together, from a purely mathematical standpoint, you will likely be better off getting the home in your partner's name as the interest rate will be lower.

Q MY BOYFRIEND/GIRLFRIEND HAS BOUGHT A HOUSE AND I AM MOVING IN. HOW SHOULD WE SPLIT EXPENSES— SHOULD I PAY PART OF THE MORTGAGE AND OTHER BILLS?

There are many factors to take into consideration here, not the least of which is how much money each of you makes relative to one another. In general, it is safe to say that if you were living in an apartment on your own, you would pay rent and utilities. If you move in with someone who has a mortgage, you could conceptually view contributing to the mortgage and utilities the same way.

However, since you would not be building any "equity" in the home, we'd strongly caution you against paying for any "capital improvements" to the house (unless you go to the substantial step of coming to some sort of written, legally binding understanding of how you would be compensated if the two of you split up).

Q MY BOYFRIEND/GIRLFRIEND LIKES TO "LIVE LARGE" BUT I'M
STRUGGLING TO KEEP UP. WHAT SHOULD I DO?

In a situation where two people are dating, and they have very different incomes and spending habits, it is more important than ever to Get Financially Naked. For instance, you may tell your partner something as blunt as, "I make $50,000 a year, have $22,000 in student loans, and $7,000 in credit card debt. I love you and I love doing things with you, but I also want to be financially responsible. As you can see with these figures, I can't afford the lifestyle you lead. I see two choices. We can either adopt a more thrifty lifestyle for the things we do together, or you can pay for the things I feel I can't afford."

When partners have totally different views when it comes to money (and this is very common), it's typically not an easy conversation. If you get push back, we'd recommend really assessing whether this is an issue you are willing to work through with your partner. While love is powerful, so too is the pain of financial angst. It is not fair to you to be expected to spend beyond your comfort point.

Q HOW DO MY BOYFRIEND/GIRLFRIEND AND I KEEP UP WITH THE WEDDING MADNESS AROUND US? IT SEEMS LIKE THERE ARE COUNTLESS WEDDINGS TO ATTEND—AND ALL THE PRESENTS AND TRAVEL COSTS ARE REALLY ADDING UP.

Since it has truly become a "world gone wild" when it comes to weddings these days, we'd recommend dealing with the madness in a non-traditional way. Specifically we suggest each of you take a deep breath and write down—from your heart— how you'd like to resolve the situation. Then exchange the papers and read each other's response out loud (the purpose of writing down and exchanging is to keep you from getting cold feet about saying what you really think). You may decide that it is based on whose friend is getting married, split 50/50 every time, or split proportionally relative to each of your incomes. There is no right or wrong way to decide who pays for what. The key is for you two to talk about what each of you wants and come to an arrangement that you both feel good about.

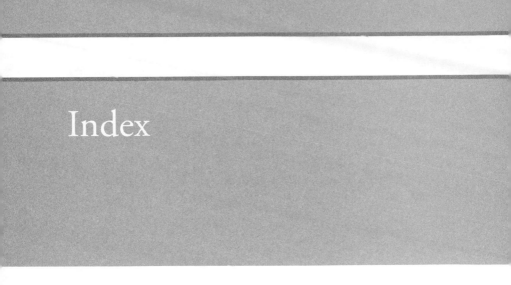

Index

G

I

H

M

ACKNOWLEDGMENTS

First and foremost we thank our husbands—for their unwavering support, encouragement, and cheerful willingness to eat canned food while we feverishly worked away on this manuscript. Without them, literally and figuratively, this book would not have been written.

A joint thanks to our literary agent, Bill Gladstone, for believing in us and in this project from day one. The same goes for our energetic editor, Chelsea King, Karen Cooper, Beth Gissinger, Chris Duffy, and the entire Adams Media family. A special big thanks to Meryl Moss on the PR front, who has worked tirelessly since our first book, *On My Own Two Feet*, to help us establish the kind of national platform that will enable as many people as possible to be helped by our books. To Saul Kessler, web guru extraordinaire, we think of you every single time we look at the beautiful website you designed for us. To Ellen Foreman, for your willingness to help us meet our deadline with such good cheer. To Ira Epstein, Steve Fassler, and Greta Drennan for helping round out the Two Feet LLC team. We both wish to thank Frank, Frank, and Mike for their incredible support of our financial literacy advocacy efforts. And last, but absolutely not least, to all of our friends who supported us every step of the way on this journey. We started to list you all out by name, and it became comical—we are blessed to know such an extensive cadre of kind spirits that it was turning into a whole chapter of thanks. You know who you are. We are sending each and every one of you a karmic hug and vow to pay your kindness forward by helping as many people as we can with this work.

Manisha extends an extra special thanks to her family: her amazing husband Randy McClahanan, her loving parents Haren and Barbara Thakor, and her brilliant brother Sunil Thakor.

Sharon extends an extra special thanks to her family: Without her wonderful husband Greg Maged, this book would not have been possible. Sharon also thanks her parents Tamar and Raphael Kedar and siblings Eyal Kedar and Iris Rubin.

ABOUT THE AUTHORS

Manisha Thakor and Sharon Kedar are on a mission to help people live their lives from a position of financial strength. They are particularly interested in helping people who want to take charge of their financial situation, but find the details of personal finance B-O-R-I-N-G. Best they can tell, that's 90 percent-plus of people. When asked to describe their books, they like to say they are, "Personal finance books for people who don't like personal finance." The magic of their partnership is their yin and yang when it comes to this subject. Manisha is part of that 10 percent (or less!) of the population who thinks personal finance is the most exciting subject ever. Sharon is much more representative of the rest of the population in that she fully recognizes how important this topic is . . . but finds the details mind-numbing. This unique combination is what has enabled Manisha and Sharon to write personal finance books that tell you what you need to know without boring you to tears.

Coauthors of the short, fun guidebooks *Get Financially Naked: How to Talk Money with Your Honey* and *On My Own Two Feet: A Modern Girl's Guide to Personal Finance*, Manisha and Sharon are also best girlfriends with over twenty years of combined experience in the financial services industry. At various points in their careers, they have worked as financial analysts, portfolio managers, and client servicing/marketing executives for leading investment management firms with billions of dollars in assets under management.

Both Manisha and Sharon earned MBA degrees from Harvard Business School and are chartered financial analyst (CFA) charter holders. Manisha received her BA in American Studies from Wellesley College and lives with her husband in Houston, Texas, and Santa Fe, New Mexico. Sharon received her BA in Economics from Rice University and lives with her husband and children in San Francisco, California.

Manisha and Sharon's financial literacy advocacy work has been featured in such publications as the *New York Times, Business-Week, US News & World Report, Glamour, Real Simple, Woman's Day,* and *Essence.* Manisha and Sharon are also frequent guests on TV and radio shows around the country including CNN's *Your Bottom Line,* CNBC's *Power Lunch,* NBC's *Nightly News,* NPR's *51%—The Women's Perspective,* and *Oprah & Friends Radio.* Learn more at their website, *www.GetFinanciallyNaked .com.* As Manisha and Sharon like to say of their work, "More Than a Book—It's a Movement!"